AMERICAN ENGLISH,
Italian Chocolate

AMERICAN ENGLISH, Italian Chocolate

SMALL SUBJECTS OF GREAT IMPORTANCE

RICK BAILEY

University of Nebraska Press | Lincoln & London

Acknowledgments for the use of copyrighted
material appear on pages 207–8, which constitute
an extension of the copyright page.

∞

Library of Congress Control Number: 2017938202

Designed and set in Fournier MT Pro by L. Auten.

For Tizi, Lisa, and David

CONTENTS

AMERICAN ENGLISH,
Italian Chocolate

1

Big White Birds

I'm not supposed to see this: a woman is stopped behind me at an intersection, cell phone pressed to her face, her free hand chopping the air while she gives someone what for. This sunny Tuesday morning in June, the grass is green, the trees are in full, gorgeous leaf, and the woman's face is breaking into jagged pieces as she pours out her anger. I fix my mirror, the better to see her. It's a private moment, but I can't help but watch because some years ago, on this very corner, my wife and I were having such an argument, and I was chopping the air too, a grotesque mask of anger on my face, and we were being watched.

But on that day my wife was in the car with me, and the person watching was beside us, not in front of us, watching us with a bemused look on her face, not unlike the look on my face right now. When I stopped fulminating and took a breath, my wife turned and looked out the window at the woman spectator.

She jerked a thumb in the woman's direction. "What's that bitch looking at?" she said.

The light changed, and we both burst out laughing, which meant whatever the conflict was, in all likelihood, we were going to get through it.

When the light changes, things are getting worse for the woman behind me. I drive through the intersection, watching her complete a left turn. Then I see it: a male mallard standing by the side of the road. Never a good sign. I slow down and see, flattened on the centerline, a female duck. But for the orange feet, it looks like a savaged sofa pillow. I feel this tightening in my chest. Who wouldn't? Who doesn't love a duck?

For a month or two every year, we have ducks in the neighborhood, in our yard, in our ditch. We have two ducks, a male and a female. We'd like to think that, like us, they mate for life. They squabble, they bully each other and shut each other out, but they hang in there and make things work. This idealized notion of duck love, it turns out, is a fantasy. Termites mate for life. Wolves and swans mate for life. Ducks do not.

We'll look out an east window of the house and see two heads bobbing in the ditch, or we'll see the two of them squeezing through the fence to get to the neighbor's bird feeder. Sometimes they sit under one of our apple trees and have a conversation. She says, "Quack." And if my sources are correct, he answers—when he does—with a soft, low-pitched, slightly uxorious "Rhab-rhab." Wherever they go, she goes first. He follows, more brilliantly colored, slightly wider, possibly dumber, possibly mesmerized by her tail. And wherever they go, they almost always walk.

Why on earth do they walk?

Why would they squeeze through a fence when they can fly over it? Why would they walk across the road? Maybe it's a relief not to fly. Flying is hard work. In seasonal migration, ducks fly fifty miles per hour at altitudes up to four thousand feet. With a fifty-mile-per-hour tailwind, they cover eight hundred miles a day, a trek so demanding they then take three to seven days to rest and feed and recover.

But in the case of these ducks, our yard ducks, my belief is they don't fly because when they fly, they don't really know where they're going. They know our yard and Beverly's yard. They've been to John's yard across the street. *Let's waddle over to Beverly's and see if she put out some of that corn.* They know the Mississippi flyway and their flight plan between here and Arkansas and Louisiana. But otherwise, I think they're pretty much lost most of the time. When they take off and get above tree level, how do they know where they're going? Do they think, *Hey, I saw some water over by the library.* Or, *Let's fly over to Drayton Plains.* I don't think so. They must think, *Where the hell are we going?* And, *Whatta ya say we head back to the ditch and chill?* It's not like they're looking for other ducks to hang out with. Unlike geese, which get mobbed up, ducks seem to pair up, find their little bowers of delight, and lie low.

We refer to these two as "our ducks." My wife refers to them as Mr. and Mrs. Mallard. We have the idea, probably ridiculous, that the same ducks come back to us year after year. Like our ditch is their Poconos, and the lovin' is easy.

So seeing the dead female, even if it's not our female (and how can I be sure?), and her swain by the side of the road, even if they don't mate for life, is a shock. I feel vicarious mallard grief.

The dead duck—and our fantasy of the two of them mating for life—reminds me of the miraculous appearance of swans in Freeland one year.

"Let's go for a ride," my father said one Sunday.

As a kid, I remember having a sense of total disorientation, usually in the car, usually at night, my father driving, my mother sitting next to him, my brother and I in the back. I would wonder, a pit of fear in my stomach, *How can we not be lost? How do they know where to go?*

We took lots of rides on Sundays, usually in the late afternoon. While my parents talked in the front seat, my brother and I looked out the car windows, hoping the ride would lead to Mooney's Ice Cream Shop in Saginaw. Some days my father would take circuitous routes to fool us, so we would have that moment of surprise when we recognized at last where we were. If we found ourselves on Brockway, that odd hypotenuse in mostly perpendicular Saginaw, we sat forward in our seats, eager for sweets. But this particular day, I knew Mooney's was not in the picture. We were going the wrong way. As I monitored our left and right turns, the farms and barns and bean fields, I got the idea we were going to Breckenridge, which should have meant a visit to my grandparents. No such announcement was made. The mood in the car was somber. My parents talked, when they talked at all, in hushed tones. Something was wrong.

We passed the road to my grandparents' house. Then came a turn I recognized, toward Henry and Kathryn's house. Henry was my father's childhood friend. They had been in the war together, Henry on a ship in the Pacific, my father operating a radio for the Army Air Force. My father was the last one to see Henry's brother Don alive. They met by accident on a train moving troops. Don had a box of fried chicken his mother had sent him. They sat on the train in the middle of nowhere, ate chicken, and talked about home and where they thought they were going. When the train reached Chicago, they said good-bye. From there my father went to Guam. Don went to Italy and was killed.

Henry was my father's age, but he looked older. He had smoker's gravel in his voice. His face was red, tracked with blue veins and broken capillaries. He had a substantial gut, spindly legs, and tattoos on his right arm. He seemed ill at ease around kids. When we swung into Henry's driveway that day and got out of the car, my father pointed at the rope swing hanging from the willow in the front yard. He told us to stay outside.

Ordinarily on a Sunday afternoon, Henry and Kathryn's son Billy came outside, and we played together. That day he did not. Billy wasn't there. My brother and I killed time for a while. We took turns on the swing. We threw rocks at frogs in the ditch. Finally we went inside to ask, politely but firmly, still thinking of Mooney's, when we were going to get out of there.

My mother was sitting on the sofa in the living room with Kathryn, whose face was red and distorted, her eyes swollen from crying. My father was at the kitchen table talking to Henry. When he said something quietly to him, I saw Henry sit back, shaking his head, and blow a stream of blue smoke at the ceiling.

We were given a few vanilla wafers and ushered back outside. A few minutes later my parents came out of the house and pulled the door shut behind them. We rode in silence back to Saginaw, went to Mooney's, and got ice cream.

On the ride home I crunched on my cone. My brother, two years older and a better listener, leaned over and whispered in my ear, "Henry has a woman."

"Huh?" I said. "A what?"

He put his finger to his lips. "A woman," he said. "Henry's got a girlfriend."

I couldn't make sense of it. How could Henry have a girlfriend? I looked at my parents, at the space between them in the front seat of the car. Had my mother, I wondered, ever sat over there right next to him in the car? Had they once held hands? I'd seen them all dressed up and dancing together at a social function one night and found it to be funny and embarrassing. What were they doing? The thought of them having a life separate from each other had never occurred to me. Nor had it occurred to me that they could ever want to be with anyone else. Every night, after they turned the lights off, I heard them kiss each other and say good night. Five kisses.

"Good night, sweetie."

"Good night, dearie."

When I came downstairs the next morning, they were up already, in the kitchen, being parents.

Henry, Kathryn. A woman.

My father sat up straight in the car, as usual, but that day he seemed a little smaller, like something had crumbled inside of him. We seemed vulnerable.

Sometime after that, there was a small commotion in town. It had rained hard for a week straight. The Tittabawassee River had risen above its banks and flooded the flats on both sides of the river. Word traveled: there were swans west of town. On the next Sunday afternoon we got in the car, drove across the bridge, and stopped on the west side of the road, joining a throng of people looking out over the flooded remains of a cornfield. A hundred yards out, two swans swam in the brown floodwater. My mother had brought binoculars. We took turns looking at them.

"Where do you think they're going?" someone asked.

No one knew. We just hoped they would stay and maybe come a little closer. When it was my turn, I held the binoculars to my face and brought the birds into focus. All the buildup. They were kind of a disappointment. What was the fuss? They were just big white birds.

The next day they were gone. A week later the floodwaters had receded. In the stretches of river water left in low sections of the field, carp flopped around, slowly suffocating. As far as I know, the swans never came back.

2

Boy Scouts, Ringworm, and Paris

I came perilously close to going to a two-week Boy Scout camp. My brother had gone a couple of times. It seemed natural that I would go too. I liked swimming, I liked tents and knives, I liked tying knots. But all that stuff about medals and badges, about merit, filled me with performance anxiety.

During the first few meetings I went to, in the school gym, we all stood in line a lot. At attention. We saluted a lot. We saluted no one in particular. The salute was like a toast, To Scouting!

We recited the Boy Scout pledge: "Something something something, brave, clean, and reverent." One Tuesday night I had to fold the American flag with Mike George. Actually, I had to do it *for* Mike George. He had rank—I think he was a lieutenant. It was our nation's flag, deserving of our respect, I got it, but he was so pious and grim about it, glaring at me like the flag was going to be part of a funeral—my funeral if I didn't do it right—that scouting just did not make a good first impression. Reverent was a reach for most of us in that room. Don't get me started on clean.

I went to a cookout one Saturday in Wardine's Woods to earn my cooking badge. ("Cookout" was not the official Scout term. I think Lieutenant George called it a bivouac.) The Tenderfoots—not

Tenderfeet—had to use pathetic aluminum mess kits to rustle up grub over an open fire. No hot dogs allowed. I remember looking at Reed Leman's chow. He was poking at some meat sizzling in the pan. He told me it was turtle.

His brother Glen said, "Yeah, turtle."

"Where'd you get it?" I asked.

Reed said they'd caught it and killed it, just a few minutes ago. Now they were cooking it.

His brother Glen said, "Yeah, killed it."

I warmed up some ground beef, gave my potatoes a bath in a panful of not-hot water, and burned my fingers. Mike flunked me on account of the potatoes, while Reed Leman passed with flying colors. His potatoes were covered in savory turtle gravy. His brother Glen said, "Yeah, gravy."

That February, still a Tenderfoot, I spent one miserable night at Bear Lake, a "polar bear" event. Before going outside to sleep in tents in subzero temperatures, we sat in the mess hall eating chicken neck soup that the dads ("masters" in scout parlance) had prepared. My tentmate, Howdy Richards, had three bowls, spitting out vertebrae like dice as he ate. The masters announced they would sleep inside, in case we needed them. Mike George made ready to sleep in a hole he dug in the snow. When Howdy and I trudged out to our pup tent, all I could think was, *What's good about this?*

And now, the summer of my twelfth year, I was going to spend two full weeks at Bear Lake?

That's when ringworm came to visit.

I was thinking about ringworm the other day, waiting at the gate to get on a plane in Paris, where I had amused my bouche for a week. A twenty-something woman sat down across from me. She had red Lady Godiva hair and a red passport. She wore a gray jumper, black stockings, and knee-high black leather boots. I had decided to stop reading *A Movable Feast*—figuring I didn't really need it anymore—and to wait patiently instead. I would enjoy a moment of vacancy and watch people.

This woman took out her computer, turned it on, and began to read. While she read, she groomed herself. She braided her red hair into red rope and threw it over her right shoulder. Then she went to work on her face. She scratched at blemishes on her cheeks, above her eyebrows, and on her chin. Every so often she would purse her lips left, pinch a pimple on her right cheek, and pull a cone of flesh from her face, stretching it, holding it, then stretching it farther, to the breaking point. When the cone snapped back in place, she looked from her computer to her thumb and forefinger, rolling something between them, evaluating each specimen of human matter she had harvested before letting it fall to the airport carpet. I couldn't take my eyes off her.

She reminded me of a boy I used to watch during church services when our kids were small. He picked and scratched at himself through the service. For some reason, his mother favored the front row, so the entire congregation could watch him while he inspected and then ate every bit of organic crud he scraped from his flesh. Before having a bite of Christ, this little manimal served himself *himself* as an appetizer.

When it was announced the flight would be delayed, the red-haired woman was swatting her left ear. The action reminded me of a duck I'd seen in the yard, whacking its ear with a giant orange foot.

The summer I was to go to Boy Scout camp, I noticed a red spot the size of a dime on my belly. It looked like a sunspot, its circumference raised and fiery red, the interior a crater of glowing pink-orange. It didn't hurt or itch. It was just there. Then I noticed one on my neck. After a day or two, a few more spots appeared on my arms. When I showed my mother she took me to the drugstore and consulted

Fred Gaul, the pharmacist. He looked and thought, looked again, and then said, "Hmmm."

"And here's a new one," my mother said. I felt her tap the top of my head.

Fred said, "Mhmm hmmm."

I squirmed a little. Time was wasting. I had to make the most of my summer before going to camp.

Fred nodded sagely and said, "I'd take him to the doctor, Alice."

When we got home from the drugstore, my brother pointed out that the dog had spots on its belly just like mine. At the dinner table that night there ensued a debate between my mother and father about whether I had infected the dog or it had infected me. When I scratched one of the spots on my belly, my father told me not to pick at it and to go wash my hands.

A week passed before I went to the doctor. In the meantime, the multiplication of spots seemed to stop. The ones on my arms, legs, and torso were just there. But the one on my head grew to the size of a quarter, then a silver dollar, then the circumference of a coffee cup. Where it grew, my hair fell out. I began to look like a friar preparing to take orders.

Our family doctor referred me to a dermatologist named Dr. Hand. My mother drove us into downtown Saginaw, parked, and we walked the hot sidewalk to the door of an old building that opened to a narrow stairway. Our footfalls echoed in the stuffy air on the long walk up. I didn't know anything about doctors, but I was used to brightly lit spaces that smelled clean and alcoholly. What waited for me up there filled me with dread.

There was no one in the waiting room. I sat on a creaky chair and looked at a pile of *Reader's Digest*s, which reminded me that I should be reading my *Boy Scout Handbook*.

Dr. Hand was a cranky old guy. He had white hair on his head and tufts of wiry bristles growing out of his nose and ears. When he came into the examining room, he said a gruff hello to my mother and looked at me like I should have been taken to the vet. He examined my arm and belly and scratched some scales off my bald spot with what felt like a glass laboratory slide.

How long would it last? my mother wondered.

"A while," he said.

Would my hair grow back?

"Eventually," he said.

The question that interested me was who had it first, the dog or I, but I decided not to ask. Dr. Hand was not a conversationalist.

When we left, he handed my mother a white jar of salve and told her I should keep it rubbed into my scalp.

"Get him a hat," he said. "He'll need it."

She rubbed some in when we got home. The ointment was black and smelled like tar. When I went outside, the summer sun warmed it up, and droplets of the stuff trickled slowly down my neck. The next morning, I pulled a hat on, which contained the melt. By noon the hat was stained black from the salve. Friar no more. I felt marked for Satan.

The good thing was, I had a parasite in me. I might be infectious. Scout camp was out of the question.

Once we boarded, I lost track of the redhead and her busy fingers.

The flight was nine hours. I had an aisle seat in a row of three center seats. There was an empty seat between me and the lady on the other aisle. My hope was the middle seat would stay empty. I wouldn't have to get up to let someone go to the can. I wouldn't have to negotiate the issue of who claimed the narrow armrest between us.

"Is the flight full?" I asked the woman. She was French-lady thin, with a French-lady hair bob. She was dressed in jeans and an untucked button shirt that revealed—when she hoisted her bag to the overhead—an ivy tattoo on her stomach, left of her belly button, which disappeared below her beltline. It reminded me of that Botticelli woman with the garland coming out of her mouth.

"What?" She had long, slender fingers. Her arms and hands were tan. On the middle finger of her right hand, she wore four silver rings, on her thumb, a silver thumb ring.

"Do you know if the flight is full?" I said.

The look she gave me meant either *I don't understand your language* or *"What?" is the last thing you will hear me say.*

The next nine hours, she looked straight ahead, French-lady aloof, totally self-contained. She read a French newspaper, watched movies on her computer, and blew her nose.

And it was—there's no other word for it—a prodigious blow. French lady's nose blow made a deafening noise, like a spring had sprung open and mucous was squirting/spraying/geysering into her French hankie. On roughly thirty-minute intervals, she blew and blew. Once, I saw her thumb and forefinger pinch a nostril, an exploratory pick.

I would have given anything to make eye contact. *Good one*, I would have said. *You're one of us.* Some people have grotesque black bald spots. Some root out blackheads and flick them on the rug. This woman blew.

We're all full of bugs and parasites. There's no escape. We have to be brave.

3

Sound Off

On days my mother had meetings after school, someone came to stay with my brother and me until she got home. The idea was to keep us out of trouble. Tom had started a fire in a neighbor's garage one summer—a small fire, a friendly fire, pure science on his part. Nevertheless, he stood accused and was no longer above suspicion. In my case, I was caught smoking down by the river. When my father pressed me on the subject, I confessed I had stolen the cigarettes from Joe Hrcka's Mobil station down the street. But only once, I insisted. I was still in elementary school. I didn't want my parents to think they had a smoker and a petty thief on their hands, which in fact they did. An amateur liar too. Danny Leman and I, on more than a couple of occasions, had walked out of Pat's Food Center with packs of Swisher Sweets stuffed in our pants.

Thursdays the woman who cleaned our house sat with us for an hour or two. Her name was Velma Studaker. She was not quite five feet tall, a vigorous, unmarried woman of few words who dressed in brown and had a helmet of brown hair. She went to our church. She loved us and exuded a force field of rectitude. On her days I think my brother and I stayed straight just to save her the agony of having to rat on us.

Other afternoons our unlikely companion was Mrs. Mack. She lived across the street with her daughter, Marge, who had two children—one a rangy teenager who got in a lot of fights (his nickname was Mugs), the other a daughter who had been crippled by polio and sat in a wheelchair. Mrs. Mack was an unlikely choice because it was clear to anyone who spoke to Marge that there was alcohol in the house, a lot of it, and most definitely the hard stuff. My parents did not drink. They didn't socialize with people who drank. We avoided restaurants that served alcohol. But on those afternoons my parents needed someone, Mrs. Mack crossed the street, climbed the steps on our back porch, and came in the house.

Unlike Velma, there was an air of fatigue and anger about Mrs. Mack. She sat in a wing chair in the living room, stiff and immovable, and watched *As the World Turns* and *The Merv Griffin Show*. She ignored us, except on cold afternoons when she ordered us to turn up the heat in the house. We tried to ignore her too, and we would have escaped to the swing set in the backyard if it weren't for a special talent she possessed.

During commercial breaks, she would trudge into the kitchen, take down a drinking glass, and fill it half full with water, into which she stirred a teaspoon of baking soda. Steadying herself with one hand on the kitchen counter, she raised the glass and downed her drink. Having returned to the living room, she sat and waited, ruminating, scowling at the TV. Five minutes would pass, maybe ten. Without warning she would raise the deepest, most resonant belches we had ever heard. The first time it happened I'm sure both my brother and I blushed and looked at each other, horrified, unable to believe our ears. Just about every day, unembarrassed, she eructed in our living room, delivering sonorous, roaring belches, while we hovered nearby, out of sight, within easy earshot. One time, after a particularly powerful one, she said, as if putting the matter to rest for us, "I have a heartburn."

At that age, we were still finding our voices. We would come to appreciate the difference between an accidental eructation and a purposeful one.

One day in seventh-grade math, Ellen Schmidt turned to say something to me, opened her mouth, and emitted a tiny, audible—and unmistakable—burp. She turned red; we both laughed. On the other hand, there were belches that were created, that were *willed*. While Mrs. Mack's were strictly utilitarian, and Schmidt's was accidental, these were performance burps, and they could be impressive for duration, tonality, and, of course, volume. Two classmates I remember were particularly eloquent.

Many mornings after our family moved out of town, Mark Trogan and Dan Leman picked me up in the red pickup truck the Trogans used for utility purposes in their hotel and restaurant business. Sometimes driving back to town on our way to school, listening to Paul Revere and the Raiders on the radio, we took turns belching. Mark was the boss. There was no dispute. He produced numbers that were long, rounded, and ear-splitting. He had a wide mouth, which he opened and stretched to ensure maximum fullness of sound.

Mark was bested, to my knowledge, only by Bob Strecker. If a belch could have a kick or thrust, Bob's did. When he squared his shoulders and let one go, his lips forming a tight, perfect O, the sound and the force of it were worthy of a physics experiment, for which, unfortunately—this being the predigital age—we lacked the technology. I'm sure the data would have been impressive.

Scientists have taken little interest in belching. The *American Journal of Gastroenterology* makes mention of "a behavioral peculiarity," offering this clinical distinction: "The gastric belch is the result of a vagally mediated reflex leading to relaxation of the lower esophageal sphincter and venting of gastric air. The supragastric belch is *a behavioral peculiarity*. During this type of belch, pharyngeal air is sucked or injected into the esophagus, after which it is immediately expulsed before it has reached the stomach" (my emphasis). Indeed. In their study of the supragastric variety, I can just picture a team of gastroenterologists observing adolescent boys with time on their hands and easy access to air. The *Journal* adds: "Behavioral therapy has been proven to decrease belching complaints in patients with isolated excessive belching." They don't describe the therapeutic regimen, but I guess it would include grounding, withholding allowance and privileges, frequent endless lectures, and beatings.

Oddly, I have scant memory of my children learning to eructate. One child, I recall, could belch but not whistle; the other whistles but does not belch. There may be an obscure genetic determinant at work here, the way some people have, or lack, the ability to roll their tongues, or some family members have, or lack, attached earlobes.

I cannot imagine not being able to belch. The behavior is antisocial and puerile, but not without an element of joy. Maybe Mrs. Mack cracked a smile once in a while.

4

Kissing Age

Last night, halfway through *Jeopardy!*, I asked my wife if she wanted to suck face. She shook her head in disgust. "Suck face" is not our usual nomenclature.

"How about a smooch?"

No.

"A peck?"

"No."

"Buss?"

"Why do you talk that way?" She pointed at the TV. Alex Trebek was introducing Arthur Chu for the tenth time. Was there anything left to say about Arthur?

While the Double Jeopardy! categories loaded, I watched her. She saw me and refused to make eye contact. The truth is, I didn't want to kiss. I just wanted to use that expression. And I wanted to see what her reaction would be. Finally, she glanced in my direction, gave her head another dismissive shake, and told me I was a fool.

Wiktionary teaches us, as if that's really necessary, that "suck face" means "to kiss, especially deeply and for a prolonged time." *Free Dictionary* (by Farlex) suggests: "to engage in French kissing (soul kissing)." And the online *Urban Dictionary*, which I use when confronted with youthful patois and argot, defines "suck face" as "a game where you make out in the least atractive [sic] way possible."

I didn't know it was a game. Who would want to watch?

The first movie kiss was filmed by Thomas Edison in 1896. I've seen the film and the smacker. The film is a re-creation of a stage kiss from a play called *The Widow Jones*. Edison must have been prim as a director, instructing the actors not to suck face. The film runs forty-seven seconds. Blink and you will miss the kiss.

Imagine a movie today called *The Widow Jones*. The kissing would be wet and wild. Indeed, for some time now, I've been inclined to avert my gaze when people kiss in the movies or on TV. The kissing is usually so earnest and hungry, so noisy. Do they have to slurp like that? I can't watch. I do not find it attractive.

My first episode of real kissing was deep and prolonged. I was in eighth grade. My girlfriend and I attended a party in a two-car garage that had been converted into a rec room. We were eight or nine couples. We played records and milled about for thirty minutes, whereupon the lights were dimmed and we got down to serious kissing. From couches in corners, large La-Z-Boy recliners, and a few treacherous beanbag chairs came the sighs and sounds of slippery, wet mashing. Again and again that evening, I had the sensation of looking at myself from above, both participant and spectator. *So this is what it's like*, I thought.

At intermission, a female friend I was not kissing asked me how it was going. What I wanted to say was, "It's actually kind of boring."

"Does she like it?"

I told her I wasn't sure.

"Did you feel her up?"

"What?" I felt my face go hot and red. Didn't she know I was a Methodist?

Sometime after that rec room romp, a girl in our town named Lila Elembaas came down with mono, which my mother informed me was "the kissing disease." Lila was older and—I could only assume—way more advanced. Still, it was unsettling news. A few years later, when I learned to play blues harmonica, my mentor, Rod Gorski, told me not to French my harp. "You know how you kiss your mother?" he said. "The way you purse your lips?" He demonstrated: a round, tight pucker, at its center a whistle-sized aperture. "Like that," he said. "Mainly, you draw. That's where the good sound is." From that sucking kiss, soulful music.

Experts tell us that in human history, kissing is a recent development. Vaughn Bryant, an anthropologist at Texas A&M University and authority on the evolution of human kissing, thinks kissing probably happened by accident. Like other creatures, humans must have checked each other out by sniffing. Then one day Moog's lips brushed against Gorga's.

She said, "Hey, what was that?"

And he said, "I don't know, but I liked it."

They got right to work. The rest is history.

Texts of Vedic Sanskrit in 1500 BC make references to licking and "drinking moisture of the lips." In Song of Solomon, we read, "Let him kiss me with the kisses of his mouth. For thy love is better than wine." Yea, verily. The Bible says it's so. Sheril Kirshenbaum, research associate at the Center for International Energy and Environmental Policy at the University of Texas at Austin, reports that in the early twentieth century, perhaps 90 percent of cultures worldwide kissed. "With the rise of the Internet," she hypothesizes, "and ease of travel in the 21st century, it's fair to assume that nearly all of us are doing it."

None kiss better than the French, we might think, though plenty of Frenching must have been going on long before there was a France. And if kissing is their thing, why is their language so impoverished in that department? Only now, in 2017, is there a word for French kiss in *Le Petit Robert* dictionary (*galocher*), adding to, and perhaps improving upon, *baiser avec la langue* (kiss with the tongue). The British, a poetic people, call it "snogging." I'll take "suck face" over that, but that's me being patriotic.

My wife's culture is kissy. In Italy you may be called upon to greet loved ones and friends with two kisses. Remember, right cheek first. I tend to go left (I also twirl spaghetti counterclockwise), crossing the intersection diagonally, which leads to awkward moments and embarrassing collisions. This kissing dates back to Roman times. Precise in all administrative matters, the Romans distinguished between the *osculum*, a kiss on the cheek; the *basium*, a kiss on the lips; and the *savolium*, a deep, prolonged, soulful pre-French kiss.

My wife is a far better linguist than I am. She learned Latin from the nuns. But I can't imagine asking her, "Are you up for a savolium?" Maybe because it rhymes with linoleum.

She'll give me a signal. Something obvious, like, "Kiss me, you fool." And I will be there.

5

There Will Be Horses

This girl I was dating in high school decided we should go horse-back riding. We'd talked on the phone a lot. We'd gone to see a few movies. We'd made out at a couple of garage parties. Our relation-ship was moving along.

"Riding," I said.

She had friends who were very horse positive. A bunch of them had gone riding a few times before. Horses were so fun.

My experience with horses was limited. I knew them from tele-vision. I knew that, in temperament, horses were on a continuum, from Flicka to Fury.

As far as actual contact was concerned, a horse had stepped on my foot when I was a kid. We were at my aunt's house one summer. My brother and I followed our cousin Dean across the road into a field. Dean was a sophisticated twelve-year-old. He had a pack of Salems stuffed in his back pocket that day. I was keen to watch him smoke. No sooner had we climbed over the fence than the neighbors' pony came plodding in our direction. Its name was Daisy. When it stopped in our midst, I stepped away at first, due to the smell. Dean lit a crooked Salem, took a puff, and blew smoke out through his nostrils. He invited me to pet the pony. I approached the animal just as it was shifting its weight, and roughly a quarter of that weight went from the ground to my foot. Daisy was only a junior horse, but my foot hurt something awful.

"So you've ridden, haven't you?" she asked.

I had not yet learned the virtue of lying. Many times, I could have said. I was thrown recently by a stallion, I could have said, was in recovery, and might never ride again.

I told her I hadn't.

"It's easy," she said. "You'll love it."

I didn't know what her fantasies were. Along with kissing in Frank Johnson's garage, she may have dreamed of riding a horse bareback on a moonlit beach. Perhaps I figured in that tableau. All well and good. The problem was the horse.

Wasn't it enough to ride to the beach in a car?

On the appointed day I drove us in my VW to a horse barn fifty-some miles away. There we met a few more couples who, unlike me, were very pro-horse. They were relaxed, enthusiastic, even jubilant. I don't remember signing a release or taking out insurance. I do remember muttering "none" when asked about my level of experience and feeling terrified when we left the office and headed for the corral. I was hoping for a nag, a horse so spent, so totally consumed, it would have a comfortable bow in its back, sort of like an inverted camel. While my girlfriend and her pals scrambled up into the saddle, I was led to my mount, whose name was Tango. Tango was big and brown; I'm pretty sure it was female. The horse rental man handed me the reins, gave me a few tips on stopping and steering, and heaved me into the saddle. Away we went.

Or rather, away my friends went. Tango walked a hundred yards out of the parking lot and then pulled over to the edge of the trail and stopped.

I was sort of okay with this. I preferred not moving and would have been happy to dismount and give us both a rest, however undeserved. At Tango's walking speed, the saddle creaked and swayed. The situation felt unstable. And I was very high up there in the saddle, higher than it looked from the ground.

We sat there, checking each other out.

"Let's go," I finally said to Tango. I pulled the reins gently in the direction of the road. That was steering, right? We didn't go. The horse must have sensed I was afraid. It must have felt that I was totally beneath her sitting up there, not even worth the effort.

"Come on," I said. "Let's go catch up with the other horses."

On TV, riders said, "He-YAH." Or some variant of that locution. That seemed extreme to me, and risky, and—in a word—foolish. I needed a command that said: Let's just walk over there. No need to run. There's no rush.

I remembered my feet, down there in the stirrups, and gave Tango a tentative nudge in the go zone with my left foot. That did it. Tango dropped into low gear and returned to the trail. We walked for a minute. Then something terrible happened.

Tango began to trot.

Trotting is an unhappy middle zone between walking and galloping. I had no training. No one had told me what to do in the event of a trot, so I did what any ninny would do on a trotting horse: I clamped my hands around the saddle horn and hung on for dear life. And I bounced. I bounced up and down in the saddle, which must have given Tango perverse pleasure. We bounced along until we caught up with my girlfriend, who was riding back to find me. She smiled big and waved. She looked great on a horse. She looked at home.

"How's it going?" she yelled.

"Oh, fine," I said.

I pulled back on the reins, thinking we'd stop, but Tango, ever spiteful, kept right on going. We trotted past her.

"You're bouncing," she yelled after me. "You look really funny."

A whole afternoon stretched ahead of us. The experience never got any better.

On the way home I nursed my crushed kidneys and wounded pride. I also listened to some fanciful talk about the horse as a mystical animal. I knew I shouldn't let a horse come between us. I just had the feeling that sometime in the future, I was destined to revisit the indignity and terror of my first equestrian experience.

Since then, I've read my D. H. Lawrence; I've read my *Equus* and contemplated horse mystery at a comfortable distance. I get it. In a comfortable chair, I even like it. Lawrence's thwarted, unhappy protagonist Lou sees something elemental and sublime in St. Mawr: "His naked ears stood up like daggers from the naked lines of his inhuman head, and his great body glowed red with power. Almost like a god looking at her terribly out of the everlasting dark."

Exactly. And great. But who wants a god like that? And who needs everlasting dark?

I don't.

Some years later my wife and I were walking across Greenfield Village with a niece and nephew. That place, now called The Henry Ford, is named for a man who couldn't quite decide whether he preferred the nineteenth or twentieth century. While vintage motorized vehicles and horse-drawn wagons crisscrossed the tree-full lanes of the Village, we stopped next to a corral where a workhorse hung its head over the wood fence. Quite naturally, I offered my nephew a chance to meet a horse. You'd think at Greenfield Village you would find a kid-friendly animal.

The season was late fall. Joey was wearing mittens. When he reached up and stroked the horse's long muzzle, the horse must have smelled something appealing in the mitten. It opened its mouth and clamped onto Joey's right hand. They stood there a few seconds, motionless, boy and horse joined together. Then old Ned took another bite. Joey's hand was now halfway into the horse's mouth. This was not a mythological connection.

"Hey," Joey said, turning to look at me. Like, *Do something*.

"Hey!" I yelled. I began swatting at the horse's head with my gloves. It peered out at me from everlasting dark, and I whacked it a few more times, and harder, until at last it let Joey's hand go. Then it turned, presented its backside, and ambled across the paddock.

Looking back, I think I was more traumatized than Joey. All he wanted was to pet the animal. All I wanted was a little respect, just once, from a horse.

"Come on," I said, patting the boy on the shoulder. "Let's go pet a Model T."

6

Sick Wild

Elizabeth Kolbert's *The Sixth Extinction* got me thinking about frogs—the end of Paul Thomas Anderson's *Magnolia*, in particular, when frogs rain from the sky. First one goes *splat* against a car windshield, then a few more—*thunk, thunk, thunk*—fall from the night sky onto the roof and hood of the car. Then more of them bounce with a fleshy *thwap* off the sidewalk. There's nothing to prepare you for it. You watch, thinking, *My God, is it—frogs?* Then the all-out frog deluge comes, terrifying, apocalyptic, a plague visited upon a cast of miserable fakes, manipulators, and degenerates. You feel surprise mingled with horror: Terrible humans. Poor frogs.

Remember frogs?

I cut into one in tenth-grade science. Mr. Perry presided over the class. He was jocular and mean, usually on the same day, his hairline receding, leaving an arrowhead of short brown hair on top of his head. His signature move was to come up behind you during lab and tighten his grip on your neck and shoulders. It was not a massage. It was a warning. On frog day he invited us to follow him into the storeroom, where we reached into great jars—like the ones you would use to brew sun tea—full of frogs marinating in formaldehyde, their eyes wide open and staring at you.

My lab partner was Debbie Monroe. Perhaps not accidentally we also sat beside each other in typing class. I can still hear her and Kathy Jo Waite talking over the determined clacking of thirty typewriters. Every other sentence ended, *Sickening.*

I brought our frog back to our lab table, laid it on its back in a special dish, and stuck pins through its feet, its arms raised in alleluia, legs splayed.

"You do it," Debbie Monroe said.

We were supposed to find the heart. The procedure called for a scalpel, pressing it against the frog's chest and making a clean incision. I tickled the frog under its chin (no gloves) and then went to work, pressing our dull scalpel hard, then harder, and then much harder against its leathery skin, until the whole frog seemed to pop under the pressure, sending jets of formaldehyde into my face and eyes (no glasses) and all over Debbie Monroe's sweater.

I instinctively looked behind me for Mr. Perry's judgmental smile, half-expecting to feel his vise grip on the back of my neck.

"Oops," he said.

I wiped my eyes with my sleeve and pointed with the scalpel. "There," I said. "The heart."

Sickening.

I grew up playing on the Tittabawassee River's dioxin floodplain. One hundred feet behind our house, a hill fell to the flats. Standing under a canopy of cottonwood trees down there, you saw nothing but wilderness. We were kids. This was our wild. It was a sick wild, I now know. No one then had heard of dioxin, except for maybe Dow, eight miles upriver, and if they knew about it, they had decided to keep it a secret. When the brown current slowed to a crawl in the summer, we stooped at the edge of the river and looked for life. Early in the summer if you stirred the water, pollywogs fluttered and swam beneath the surface. Later we saw frogs sunning themselves on stones, resting on the dry black muck. You could barely take a step down there without disturbing a frog. We took them prisoner.

Not for pets. No one I knew kept a pet frog.

If we had a single qualm among us, none of us wanton boys admitted to it.

Years later, when I read about Mr. Kurtz's "fascination with abomination" in Conrad's *Heart of Darkness*, I felt a creepy sense of recognition and shame. We were capable of terrible things.

One year Roger Kipfmiller and I rode our bikes out west of town to Wagner's Pond after school. We took BB guns and a bucket. In ninety minutes we worked the south edge of the pond, shooting and killing frogs, until we had fifty or sixty of them in the bucket. Then we rode back into town. Roger's dad knew how to cook frog legs. We separated their legs from their bodies, peeled their green skins off their bony thighs and down over their webbed feet, and tossed the wishbones of meat into a bowl of salt water, at which point, to our surprise, the legs began to twitch and kick, one last muscle memory of trying to get away from us.

By the time we finished, I had to go home. I sort of *wanted* to go home. The truth is, I wasn't even sure I wanted to eat frog legs.

"I'll bring you some tonight," Roger said.

That night was a JV football game. I was going, but not to watch football. That summer I had smelled Valery Frost's lilac perfume at the Freeland Frontier Days. She had fluttered her eyes in my direction. We were going to meet in the bleachers, which we did, some moments after I saw Roger waiting by the concession stand. He had pulled a napkin from his pocket, unfolded it, and revealed a few remaining frog legs. They were brown; his father had breaded and deep-fried them.

Roger pushed the legs at me. "They're good," he said. "Like this." He picked one up by the foot, pushed one leg, then the other into his open mouth, and clamped his teeth down on the bones, dragging the meat off them. "Try one."

I ate one. He was right. They were good. But I regretted eating them because I knew I was going up in the bleachers looking for

Valery Frost, eager to smell her lilac perfume again, eager for her to drop something from the bleachers, which would require our going down there, together, to get it, under the bleachers. *Will she kiss a boy*, I wondered, *with frog on his breath?*

All those frogs back then: they seemed capable of spontaneous generation. Frogs in the house, in laundry tubs (my mother would shriek), in the basement, under the kitchen sink. Hearty, persistent, ubiquitous creatures, now dying off.

Kolbert reports that we are on the threshold of a sixth extinction. The last one happened some sixty-six million years ago. Probably an asteroid smashed into the earth. The coming die-off—actually it's already well under way—will be a gradual cataclysm. Honeybees are dropping in their tracks. The acidification of the oceans is causing a die-off of the coral reefs. Who knows what these extinctions will mean to the food chain? *Salon* reports, "By the end of this century, scientists believe, up to 20 to 50 percent of the plant and animal species on Earth could be gone forever."

Extinction, I was surprised to learn, is a relatively new idea. Jefferson thought that when he sent Lewis and Clark on their journey, they would see mastodons.

We're used to the idea of extinction. We're in it. We're the asteroid and the frogs. Don't look up. Look around.

7

The Man from Glad,
Car Crash, Amnesia

This really happened.

One Saturday night the spring of my junior year in high school, I was working until closing time at my father's gas station. At 9:30 we would raise the hoist, wet the floor, and sprinkle a pungent, yellow granular cleanser all over it to cut grease and oil that had accumulated throughout the day. Then we mopped the bathrooms and office, brought in tires that were outside on display, and emptied garbage cans on the drive. Ron Fritz was closing with me that night.

I was about to empty the can on the front island of pumps when I noticed a car stopped at our town's one stoplight. It was a pale-green Studebaker Lark. I remember its rusted door panels. I also remember the left rear of the car sagged so much I wondered if the tire were flat or the springs were broken. Just sitting there, the car began to rock, first gently, then violently, like there was a wrestling match going on inside. I was about to turn away when the light changed to green. The driver revved the engine two or three times, and the Lark wheezed through the intersection, trying to accelerate, until the car's brake lights flickered on and off, then on again. The driver slowed and swerved toward the right shoulder, the right rear door swung open, and a person spilled out of the moving car and tumbled across the pavement. The flailing arms and legs made me think at first it was a dummy.

The car kept going, disappearing into darkness around the bend in the road north of town. The person lay there on the shoulder. I thought he must be injured, maybe even dead. But after a few seconds, he stood up. I saw now it was a man. He dusted himself off, checked his moving parts, and limped off in the direction of the parking lot behind the bank on that corner.

Inside the gas station, Ron was hosing down the floor. I told him what I saw.

"No way," he said.

Not much happened in our town. We'd had a murder and a plane crash, but too long ago for us to feel the impact.

"Wish I'd seen it," he said.

We closed the gas station that night, watching for the man, both thrilled and worried that he might come back, that we might have witnessed some skullduggery and were now involved in its sinister aftermath. Before we turned the key in the door, one of us had to walk a locked bag containing the money and the day's receipts across the street to the night deposit box at the bank, an action always fraught with minor drama. After some discussion, I decided to make the drop. I crossed the street, avoiding the spot where the man had rolled out of the car. At the deposit box the keys jingled nervously in my hand while I opened it. I stuffed the bag inside and then closed and locked the box in one fluid motion. I couldn't help but turn and look behind me as I crossed the street.

Nothing further happened. At 10:00 p.m. we killed the lights and locked the doors.

It was Ron's turn to drive. We climbed into his '55 Chevy and rode into Saginaw listening to the Amboy Dukes on 8-track, arguing about UFOs. I had seen one; he had not.

Memory is capricious, frequently a liar.

Recently my brother reminded me of an event from our childhood. It was the summer of 1957. The Mackinac Bridge was under construction, an engineering feat that must have appealed to our father's imagination. We took a family trip four hours north, boarded a ferry, and motored a few miles out into the Straits. The two giant bridge towers had been erected on footings poured in 120 feet of water. They rose 550 feet in the air. The piers, cables, and catwalk were all in place. That summer, trusses were being lifted and positioned to provide the framework for the roadway. It would have been cold on the water, probably windy and rough. The bridge project must have been an awesome sight. I have no recollection of it.

I was four years old at the time, a timid child, so I'm sure this whole adventure was terrifying. Maybe that's why I don't remember it. But I remember other events from childhood that also must have been terrifying. My earliest recollection is standing up in a hospital crib and bouncing up and down while holding my groin, which was bandaged from hernia surgery. I was probably around two years old. At that time parents walked off and left their children in hospitals. Sleepover, in order to comfort the child, was not an option the way it is today. I think I was given a stuffed animal and told to buck up. I must have been traumatized being left alone like that. Around this age, I also remember sitting alone in the sandbox in the backyard of our house in town. While I played, a big black dog trotted up to me. Its head was the size of a large ham. It thrust its giant muzzle into my face, sniffed me, and then ran off. It was an archetypal visitation, an encounter with a strange black beast, and I remember it as if it happened yesterday. Why do I remember these moments and not hundreds of others, among them being on the water of the Straits of Mackinac?

Another childhood memory: waking up in my father's arms as he carried me into a strange house at night. I'm pretty sure it was the home of a relative, probably his Aunt Clarice, but as I've replayed the memory over the decades, it has shifted. I now wake up in my father's arms in the home of Danny Leman, my neighbor and childhood friend. It is a place I got to know some years after the event in question. In this finished memory, I see the sofa I knew, the front door and stairway. It even smells like Danny Leman's house. Memory has mixed things up, providing me with the wrong setting for the visit, but the recollection feels true nonetheless.

Sometime after the man fell—or was pushed—out of that car, I began to notice a figure skulking around town. He was old enough to be someone's father. He wore khakis, a light-blue Oxford shirt, and a navy blue jacket he kept zipped up. He had a thin, serious face, pointed features, and wavy gray hair. I saw him in front of Rodeitcher's Chinese Restaurant. I saw him on the sidewalk across from the coffee shop, walking with a determined gait past Al Roberts's market and Howard Schaffer's barbershop. He would pause, look behind him, and then resume his jerky, agitated walk.

Every day after school that spring, a group of us gathered in the coffee shop to drink cokes, eat French fries, and play Led Zeppelin on the jukebox. Before long others also noticed the skulker. Dennis Vickroy pointed out his uncanny resemblance to a character on television, in the commercial for Glad Wrap. He looked like the Man from Glad.

What did he want? Why was he there?

I began to wonder if he was the one who had fallen out of that car, thinking that in his fall, he had sustained a head injury and lost his memory.

When I proposed my amnesia theory, Dennis took a long drag on a cigarette and considered it. "Maybe," he said. "But then why is he antisocial? Wouldn't he ask questions? Wouldn't he want to know who he is?"

I said he might be right. Still, with amnesia—based on what I knew from TV and the movies—you could never tell.

Dennis tapped a cigarette ash on his plate. "I say he's here on an errand. It looks like he's waiting for someone."

We took turns wondering out loud about this stranger.

"Where did he come from?"

"He's a drifter."

"He looks dangerous."

"He's on the run from the law."

"Where does he sleep?"

"He's a thief."

"He's a secret agent."

"He's an assassin."

Dennis took a last drag on his cigarette and extinguished it in a puddle of catsup left on his plate of fries. "He is the Man from Glad," he said. "He's here to help keep our sandwiches and leftovers fresh."

One day when five or six of us were pressed into a booth, the Man from Glad came in the coffee shop and sat in the booth closest to the front door. He sat with his back to us, facing the sidewalk and street. When the waitress took his order, he practically shouted it at her. I wondered if he had both hearing loss and memory loss. While we watched him, Led Zeppelin's "Communication Breakdown" blared on the jukebox. Doug Propp had figured out how to turn the jukebox volume up. Once or twice, the Man from Glad turned in his seat and glared at us. When the song stopped playing, we all fell silent, watching.

"Man from Glad," Dennis said, barely audible.

Everyone at the table hunched down and snickered.

"Man from Glad," he said again, louder this time.

If he heard us, the Man from Glad didn't let on.

The internal gizmo in the jukebox clunked, and its needle lowered to a 45, more Zeppelin. We sat listening, watching. When the song ended, we all stood up and flung ourselves at the door, where we piled up like so many nervous, chuckling idiots. We couldn't resist turning to look at him. The Man from Glad was having black coffee. On the table next to his cup were a pen and a blank piece of paper. He looked up at us and yelled, "What do you goddam kids want?"

"Are you the Man from Glad?"

"Get the hell out of here," he barked at us. "Leave me alone."

The Man from Glad remained a shadowy figure around town for a few more days and then disappeared. Whatever it was, his mission was completed. I liked to think of him getting into a car at the edge of town and speeding away. In fact, I pictured his exit as a rewind of sorts: the rusty Lark backing into town from the north, the Man from Glad rolling backward, arms and legs flailing, falling back into the car as the right rear door opened and closed upon him.

And away he went, his memory intact.

For some time now I've been having premonitions.

I will be backing my car out of the garage when I anticipate, all in a flash, the entire structure caving in on the car. Or, while waiting for coffee in a Starbucks, I'm visited by the vision of the place exploding. Only it's not a vision—that suggests a scene more fully realized and protracted than these flashes are. And it's nowhere near as precise as the house falling on top of me. In a blink, I think I've known, or will know, sudden obliteration. The premonition experience lasts less than a second. It's always catastrophic.

I have an idea this is not really a premonition but a postmonition, the recovery of a memory.

The fall of 1971 I was in a serious car accident. I attended the local community college, preparing for a career in public accounting. Driving my Volkswagen across sections of farmland one morning on my way to class, I cruised through an open intersection. Tall corn grew on three out of four corners, which also made it a blind intersection. I was in the middle of this intersection when a van coming from my left collided with my car, which rolled like a yellow ball through a shallow ditch and eventually came to rest in the vegetable garden of one Mrs. Metevier. She saw everything, called for help, and was able to give an exact account of what had happened. I have no recollection of the accident, nor do I remember the day before, the morning leading up to, or the week that followed the accident.

Gradually I woke up, finding myself in a hospital bed, in traction, immobilized. I experienced the confusion—that baffling sense of disorientation and strangeness—one feels when awakened from a deep sleep. Rather than passing in a few moments, however, it lasted a few days. Nurses told me where I was. My parents, borrowing from Mrs. Metevier, explained what had happened. My legs were broken. I'd had a bad bump on the head. I began to piece together the story of that morning and the days that followed.

That happened to me? Really?

Had I been out, I wondered, unconscious for days?

It was more like a semiconscious state, my parents said. They asked me questions, and I answered in gibberish.

Did I even know who I was?

They said it was hard to tell at first.

In his 2001 memoir, *Uncle Tungsten*, Oliver Sacks recalls two events in his life that illustrate the complex relationship of trauma and memory. In the winter of 1940–41, while London was under bombardment during the Blitz, a one-thousand-pound bomb fell very near Sacks's home. The bomb didn't explode. It was the middle of the night. He and his family, along with the entire neighborhood, got out of bed and—still in pajamas—walked gently away from their homes and neighborhood, convinced that the bomb might explode any minute. (It didn't.) The second memory also involves a bomb, this one an incendiary device that did actually detonate behind their house during the war. Sacks recalls his father and brothers pumping and carrying buckets of water, pouring them, to no avail, on the fire.

It wasn't until the publication of his memoir that Sacks learned from an older brother that while the first memory was an accurate account of what had happened to him, the second one, though also accurate, was an acquired memory. At the time the second bomb struck, Sacks had already been relocated from London to the countryside, the way many youngsters were. He learned of the thermite bomb from an older brother's account of it in a letter. Over time, Sacks had taken possession of the story. He had become an eyewitness. It had become his memory, part of his life story.

"All of us 'transfer' experiences to some extent," Sacks writes, "and at times we are not sure whether an experience was something we were told or read about, even dreamed about, or something that actually happened to us." An individual's personal truth, his or her core sense of self, can be founded on both actual, verifiable events and on acquired, altered, or even fabricated events. Sacks asserts, "Some of our most cherished memories may never have happened—or may have happened to someone else."

I stayed in the hospital three weeks, fastened at first to a circle bed. The contraption was like an indoor carnival ride. I lay on my back. Every so often a nurse latched a thin board and mattress just above me to the bed frame, and the bed rotated and deposited me on my belly. Then after a while it rolled back and returned me to my original position. Once my condition improved I was moved to a regular bed. Day and night, nurses swished around me in their crisp whites. I sipped water through crooked hospital straws. I peed in a can and pooped in a pan. I looked forward, unembarrassed, to daily baths given to me by female nurses roughly my age whose touch was gentle and impersonal and sure. I woke at night and knew where I was. I waited eagerly for the bland scrambled eggs, the meatloaf, and the fruit cups when the food cart arrived. I was returning to my broken body, discovering my altered self.

In the bed next to mine was a boy my age waiting for scoliosis surgery. He was small in stature, pale and fleshy. He had a round face and a head of thick black hair. Afternoons when his friends came to visit, they huddled around his bed and talked in low voices. It was impossible not hear their stories.

They broke into houses and stores. It sounded like a hobby of theirs. They talked about their fresh loot: cowboy boots, a reel-to-reel tape deck, a glass fishbowl full of souvenir matchbooks from places around the country (all those memories!). They said they were waiting for my roommate to come back, to join them again in these heists.

When he asked me one day about myself, I said something about college and public accounting. Only a few weeks had passed since the crash, but that version of myself felt like a story now. He wondered when I would walk again. I said it would be months.

"How many?"

"Four or five."

He explained they were implanting a rod in his spine. He hoped it would help him straighten up and grow taller. I tried to picture him bigger, stronger, breaking through the back door of someone's house with a gunnysack over his shoulder and carrying off people's stuff.

"What happened?" he said.

I told him what little I knew about the morning, the collision, and what had happened next. Then, for good measure, I added, "I had amnesia."

He turned with his whole body and looked at me. "Cool," he said.

Having said it, I felt strangely enhanced. It *was* cool. No one I knew had ever had amnesia. Probably no one he knew. Then I thought of the Man from Glad, his mysterious wanderings around town, his crabby disposition. "Yeah," I said. "Just for a week or so. It was pretty strange."

"What was it like?"

I described it as if I remembered it. "You don't know where you are," I said. "You're very confused. You can't answer questions."

He turned away and thought for a minute, smoothing his thick hair. "What if it comes back?" he said. "What if you forget again?"

It never came back. And in truth, I don't really know if it was amnesia. What if it did come back? Could a person remember amnesia? Could he remember not remembering?

Shortly before leaving the hospital, I asked a nurse if I would ever recover those days before and after the accident.

"I don't know, honey," she said. "Why would you want to? What good would it do?"

No good whatsoever. But I wanted to know. One of my most important memories, I said, and it was like it happened to someone else.

"You leave it alone," she said. "You're going home. You should be glad."

Home, to my family, to my past. And to a whole future of memory that lay ahead of me.

8

Clinical

The spring I turned eighteen I took child psych at the local college. The course was my second in psychology, taught late in the afternoon by a real-world psychologist named Norval Dirksen. He wore ill-fitting suits and white stay-press shirts that floated on his two-pack-a-day frame. Between classes, while my friends shuffled data-processing cards and crunched differential equations—focusing on the hard stuff—I applied myself to my imagined future.

I memorized lists of defense mechanisms, outlined chapters in the textbook, and read *Dibs in Search of Self*, the story of an emotionally disturbed youngster who, with the help of a compassionate therapist, knits together a unified personality.

"Dibs," Dr. Dirkson said, "got better."

Around this time, we were having a situation at home. One night I woke to a heavy scratching sound on the roof. Something was up there. The sound of its claws and the hollow thump of the creature's slow footfalls just above my head filled me with the kind of primordial dread you feel only in the dead of night. I tossed the covers back, reached for pants and a shirt, and padded to the utility room, where I found my father, also partially dressed, standing in the dark testing a flashlight. "Raccoon," he said.

We opened the back door, stepped out into the muggy night, and stood in the wet grass in our bare feet. When he aimed the light at the roof, I saw he was right. A dark form huddled in one of the valleys of the roof. We took a step closer, the light jiggled, and then we stopped. The thing was looking directly at us. Its yellow eyes glowed. I knew there was no chance of it leaping from the roof and locking its teeth on my throat, but at the moment, it seemed like a real possibility. My father said he could shoot it. I pictured him aiming a rifle while I held the light. But I imagined him missing, or worse, wounding it, and the enraged animal attacking—by mistake—the guy who was holding the light. We settled on a trap, which we put next to the chimney the following morning. The next nights those yellow eyes glowed in my long-term memory. I strained to hear those terrible claws, and every morning I woke up hoping there would be nothing in the trap. I didn't want to confront it. I just wanted it to go away.

One day a week that term, I drove to a shuttered school in Saginaw, where a back room had been opened, painted cheerful colors, and dedicated to the care of emotionally disturbed children. This was what the college called "practical experience." You went to a place where a particular kind of work was done to find out if you really wanted to do it. I was watched over by a woman named Mrs. Wheeler, who told me she was actually a social worker.

She rolled her eyes. "Same thing as a psychologist," she said, "sort of."

I saw myself eventually doing couch and notebook work with "clients," but I knew I needed to start somewhere. I would have to peel a few potatoes, my father said, before I could make a soufflé.

My job was to observe. There were ten children. I watched Stephen, a round little guy with a red face who sat for hours at one of the tables swinging a wooden mallet, hammering wooden pegs into a block. And Emily, a little girl who drew black crayon swirls on tablets of paper. And Tina, who sat in a yellow beanbag chair with a doll pressed to her chest. The room was noisy. The kids cried a lot.

"Stephen says he's hot," I said one morning to Mrs. Wheeler.

"He's working," she said. She mimed his hammering motion and smiled.

"But he is hot," I said. "I touched him. He's hot."

She swung her imaginary hammer again.

The kids didn't play together much. They just collided with each other. There were frequent low-level assaults and thefts. Then they had juice.

I asked Mrs. Wheeler, "Does Tina ever leave that chair?"

Mrs. Wheeler shrugged and gave me her you'll-find-out smile.

The third week I visited there was a new boy. I assumed my point of observation and took out my notebook. This new boy, dressed in blue overalls, lay under one of the tables the whole morning. Every so often, he got up on his hands and knees, turned in circles like he was chasing his tail, and then lay back down. Surrounded by racket and chaos, he seemed nothing if not bored, taking luxurious sucks on his left thumb and stirring the hair on the back of his head with his right index finger. I ran through my list of defense mechanisms and decided to take a stab at sounding clinical.

I pointed him out to Mrs. Wheeler. "That one," I said, "seems to exhibit reaction formation."

"What?" She pushed her glasses up her nose and looked.

"Reaction formation?" I said. "His defense mechanism?"

She closed her eyes and shook her head.

I was in it. I thought I might as well formulate a complete psychological thought, put it on the table. "An exaggerated response to his surroundings, the direct opposite . . ."

"That's Patrick," she said. "He's my son."

He lay under the table on his side, his back to his mother.

"Is he . . . ?"

One look at her, and I didn't finish my psychological thought. *No, young Frankenstein, he's just visiting today*. She didn't have to say it. I gave her a tight smile and tapped my pencil a few times on my notebook.

Three more Fridays I went for this practicum. Each observation was long, loud, and uneasy. I never saw Patrick again. Mrs. Wheeler treated me with equal parts respect and newfound skepticism. Those long mornings, I think she heard what I heard—the sound of claws scratching above us, the slow progress of a creature on the roof, a beast we didn't want to catch but simply hoped would go away.

9

Psyched

Last night I had a nightmare about donuts. In the dream I was very hungry, and I was eating donuts, lots of donuts. Every donut I ate, I got hungrier. I drank down glass after glass of milk, tearing apart glazed donuts and swallowing huge chunks of them, barely chewing. Then, sort of half-asleep, half-awake, I realized it was just a dream. The sensation reminded me of what I felt when I quit smoking and then dreamed I had started smoking again. Same emotions—horror, disgust, self-loathing.

Donuts are practically a universal food. Humans must be hardwired to desire them. Donut lust lurks in our unconscious. Who came up with idea of frying dough, rolling it in sugar, pumping it full of custard, and slathering it with jam and icing and chocolate? Probably the same kind of people who thought of the lethal injection.

I was in ninth grade when Dawn's Donuts appeared on the corner of Center and Hemeter in Saginaw. I saw it as something exotic and magical that had come from outer space and landed on that corner. One happy day an ice storm blew through Freeland, uprooting trees and downing power lines. School was closed, and a bunch of us piled into Richard Roche's Chevy Nova and rode to Dawn's Donuts, where we drank mugs of coffee and ate donuts. That may have been the first time I ate a cruller, sometimes called a "French cruller."

The term "cruller," according to Free *Merriman-Webster*, comes from Middle Dutch *crul*, meaning "curl," although according to my urban dictionary, cruller also means "anus" ("yank those rosemary [*sic*] beads out of my cruller") and "a man who likes to pee on himself" ("My friend is a cruller so he always takes the stall instead of the urinal"). Very well then. But the best definition—at least the one that best harmonizes with my upbringing—is "a tractor tire–shaped donut." That pretty much nails it, while inducing fantasies of size. When I was in the ninth grade, a cruller the size of a tractor tire would have been heavenly. Or perhaps an inner tube–sized cruller, enabling a gluttonous adolescent to float down the Rifle River, yanking off hunks of donut and stuffing them in his mouth.

I was in college when Tim Hortons came along. It was the early seventies. At that time, Tim Hortons and Wendy's had not yet become a combined, multinational corporation. Tim Hortons was still a far-off Canadian thing, making it more exotic than Dawn's. I had a pal from Philadelphia named Denise who, one weekend when her friend Lynne was visiting, decided to join me on a trip to Stratford. We saw *Love's Labor's Lost* at the Shakespeare Festival and slept in pup tents in a hot, weedy lot posing as a campground, Denise and Lynne together in one tent, me solo in the other. The next morning we sat at the counter in Tim Hortons eating crullers and drinking Tim's heavenly coffee. For me, donut regret had already crept into the experience. Even one tasted like too many.

At that time my friend and her companion had a Philly pal studying art in London, so on our way back to Detroit, we stopped to visit this friend Sharon, who was older and married and had a house. To celebrate this little reunion, we did not eat donuts. We ate scrapple, a Philadelphia pork mush delicacy also known as "pon haas" by the Pennsylvania Dutch and "death by sandwich" by anyone not raised in the mid-Atlantic states. What else are you going to do with your hog offal?

It was a brief stopover, marked by an awkward moment when Sharon's husband, who wore baggy shorts and a sleeveless T-shirt and had long, shaggy hair, ushered us into the vagina room, formerly known as the dining room, to show us the latest masterpiece in his wife's oeuvre. The painting was right above the buffet and depicted a woman's thighs and gigantic sexual vortex. There was nothing stylized or abstract about it. This was no Georgia O'Keeffe flower. It was just a big anatomical billboard, in garish colors, that caused me to reflect on the difference between art (take a long look, it makes you feel good) and porn (take a quick peek, it makes you feel bad). But this thing seemed neither art nor pornography.

Denise and Lynne gazed, nodded, and approved. They said it made a statement. Sharon said that was her purpose. The feminist movement was in full swing, represented in the popular imagination by bra burning, by Gloria Steinem and her glasses, by Betty Friedan and *The Feminine Mystique*. This work of art, Sharon said, was neither aesthetic nor erotic. It made a statement.

Yeah, the Philly girls said. It's rhetorical.

We stood there in silence, sucking scrapple from our teeth, contemplating the rhetorical vagina.

"What do you think?" the husband asked me, with obvious pride. I had an idea it was not rhetorical to him.

I was at a loss. I would have been happy going back to the kitchen, even if it meant eating scrapple. Finally I just said what was on my mind: "It's really big."

Many years after that my wife and I took her cousin's family, visiting from Italy, to Disney World, where we encountered no end of food difficulty. It seemed to me, Mickey and all those roving characters notwithstanding, the place might have more properly been called Hormel Land. Hormel and its smoked, processed meat were everywhere. Breakfast in particular was a challenge. How do

Italians start the day? Sausage and eggs? No. Cereal? Don't believe those Müeslix commercials. They like coffee and pastries. Italian kids like cookies and chocolate spread. There was no chocolate spread, and none of the cookies were right anyway. The cousin's wife could find nothing to feed her child, a nervous little boy around three years old, until the second day, when she discovered sugar donuts that resembled their *bomboloni*. She broke the pastries into pieces and fed them to her boy, who lay back in her arms in dreamy donut ecstasy. What he didn't eat she finished. They had finally found a food they could reason with.

I took psychology in college. Child psychology, abnormal psychology, psychology of religion, psychology of sex. I may even have read some of Freud's *Interpretation of Dreams* and learned about the pleasure principle and wish fulfillment, about unconscious desire finding expression in dreams. The idea of dream interpretation seemed appealing. As far as I could tell, there were no rules other than "this stands for that" and "make it work." In your dream you are running. You're trying to get away from something. Those white basketballs in the dream—those are cauliflowers, which stand for your mother, who insisted you eat your vegetables. You're trying to get away from your mother.

I have an idea what Freud would have said about my donut dream, about donuts in all their various permutations. He might have been right. These days, I can't drive by Tim Hortons and not think about rhetorical vagina. But am I really working through unconscious turmoil and wish fulfillment? I don't think so. For one thing, deep down, I'm a very superficial person. And for another, to paraphrase Freud, sometimes a donut is just a donut.

10

Love and Breakup in
the Time of Watergate

My junior year of college I had a close call. I was driving home from
school one Friday afternoon, having pulled an all-nighter studying
for a test. The class was psychology of sex. I'd had a lot of psych
by that time, but not a lot of sex. I needed one more psychology
class for a minor, and then I was done. But I still kind of hoped,
as one hopes of all psych classes, that this last class would give me
some answers.

I was going home that weekend because the trio I played in had a
Friday and Saturday night gig at the Red Fox Bar. I was also going
home to see a girl named Suzanne. I wanted to find out if she and
I had a thing.

I was an hour up the road from campus that afternoon when I
realized I was in trouble. It was a damp Michigan day in October,
sky the color of slag. Three or four times my head dropped and
snapped back up, and I realized each time—with horror—that I had
been asleep for a few seconds. North of Flint, I pulled into a truck
stop and ordered breakfast. Morning food, I thought. I knew my
Pavlov. I had eggs and potatoes and drank a lot of coffee. Awake
and face the day. Thirty minutes later, on the business loop through
Saginaw, driving with the windows down and my shoes off and the

AM radio volume turned up, I started to nod off again. It's a curvy stretch of road. The last thing I heard before my car crossed lanes heading for the median was the Singing Nun's folked-up version of "The Lord's Prayer."

I grazed the guardrail at fifty per. The car ricocheted back onto the road, and I jerked awake.

The singing nun was still singing when I crossed back into the right lane and pulled onto the shoulder to stop and assess the damage. I was trembling, both frightened and relieved. I got out of the car and took a few huge gulps of cool air. *Good Lord*, I thought, *I am an idiot.*

A few minutes later, I turned into the driveway at home, where I was met by my father. I explained to him what had happened.

"Really," he said, shaking his head. "The Lord's Prayer?"

The driver's side door screeched when I opened and closed it. I remember thinking, looking at that savaged door panel and trim: *How'd the door handle not get swiped off?*

"It's a miracle," he said.

"Yes, it is," I said.

The idea was Suzanne would meet me at the bar that night, hear the band, and we would talk between sets. I went in the house, took a shower, and called her.

"That's tonight?" she said. "I have to work. I'm subbing for Delphine."

"Well," I said, "what about tomorrow night?"

"Tomorrow night too." She waited tables at the Lil Chef. Delphine had gallbladder trouble and a sick kid. Suzanne said she was sorry.

I told her it was okay. I kind of wanted to talk. The bar wasn't exactly ideal for, you know, *talk* talk.

"*Talk* talk," she said. "That sounds serious."

I told her I had driven off the road on the way home and hit a guardrail. I felt kind of shook up. Plus, you know, what were we doing?

"How about Sunday?"

I had to get back to school on Sunday, but I was motivated. "What about breakfast?" I said. "How would that be?"

She and I had met that summer in an American lit class I was taking at the local community college. The instructor was old and stuffy and gentle and kind of drunk on literature in a way I was starting to admire. One day Suzanne came in and sat next to me. She wore jeans and a white muslin shirt with the sleeves rolled up above the elbow. The top two buttons on the shirt were undone. The jeans and shirt were tight. I noticed there were other vacant seats in the room. She had sat next to me on purpose.

We heard about the Over-soul and friendship and self-reliance for half an hour. We went over some passages from Emerson and then took a break. I followed Suzanne out of the classroom. She leaned back against the wall in the hallway and crossed her arms, waiting. It was my move.

"So," I said, "what are you into?"

She gave me an amused look.

"You know," I said. I tried to embellish the question with a couple of interpretive hand gestures.

She said she was into—I'm pretty sure she gave me air quotes—the Transcendentalists. She liked Dickinson more than Whitman. She appreciated the Puritans for the diaries they kept but otherwise found them repressive. She was taking this class, she said, for a refresher. She planned to go to law school.

"What about you?"

I said I didn't know. I told her right now I was at Eastern, currently in psych, adding—when I saw the eye roll coming—that I thought I'd end up in English. It was my turn to say something about the course, to mention someone we'd read. Panicked, I said I really liked the William Cullen Bryant stuff from last week, especially the poem about the bird.

"Vainly," she said, "the fowler's eye might mark thy distant flight to do thee wrong."

"That's the one," I said. She memorized. "You memorize?"

She said it was a hobby. And did I want to come over to her house after class?

I followed her home, that day and every day for the three remaining weeks of class. We sat on the couch and made out. While we did that, we listened to Steely Dan and watched the Watergate hearings, some days both at the same time. A parade of witnesses took the stand. John Dean testified. Suzanne guided my hands. Alexander Butterfield testified. She crossed a leg over mine.

We drove north and went swimming one day. I think she wanted me to see her in a bikini. Another day, while we watched the hearings, her mother passed through the living room and went into the kitchen. She was tall and pale and—I thought—prematurely gray. She was not the least interested in us or in what we were doing.

"There's tapes of conversations in the Oval Office," Suzanne called to her. "Nixon's in a lot of trouble."

A kitchen cupboard opened and closed. Her mother floated past us again, holding a cocktail.

One afternoon I met her father when I was leaving. He had short dark hair and black-framed glasses. He reminded me of Howard Baker. I wondered if he was a lawyer.

"Nice to meet you," he said. We were standing in the doorway. There was an awkward silence. He stepped aside to let me out and then turned to Suzanne and said, "What about that Johnny?"

The Red Fox Bar was a farmer/trucker/ass-kicker bar at a four-way stop west of Chesaning, the only sign of civilization on that corner and for some miles beyond. It was run by a little woman named Rita and her disgruntled son, Dave. They paid us thirty bucks each for playing four sets a night.

Just before our first set, which started at 9:30, Rita would get in her Impala and drive home, leaving her son to mix drinks and serve up chips and jerky. He also bounced as needed. When business was slow, Dave leaned on the bar next to a vat of pickled eggs. This, he said, was not where he wanted to be. He said he really wanted to be a cop. I think bouncing was the only thing he found satisfying about the job. Busy nights he outsourced bouncing to a long-haired Mexican man named Pinto. Pinto stood at the end of the bar in a swath of shadow and glowered at patrons. He bounced for pleasure. I'm pretty sure he did it for nothing. Beating on guys made him feel good. He knew what he wanted.

Both nights that weekend I sang a couple of Beatles' songs: "You're Going to Lose that Girl" and "You Can't Do That." Every so often I'd look to the front door and imagine Suzanne walking into the bar, smiling, and waving at me. I pictured us sitting by ourselves at a corner table in the back—far from the smell of cigarette smoke, spilled beer, and urinal cakes—having a serious talk.

She never came.

My car door screeched open and closed in her driveway that Sunday morning. I think I got to her house a few minutes early.

I knocked on the door, a few polite knuckle knocks. When nothing happened, I rang the doorbell.

A light rain was falling. I stepped off the porch and looked up at the second-story windows. I checked my watch. Straight up 9:00 a.m. I knocked again, a little harder, and rang again, more insistently, starting to feel angry and a little ashamed. The doorbell in particular got me. You ring a doorbell six or seven times, how do you not feel needy and ridiculous? I rang it again. Leaning close to the door I could hear the tones behind it. I could picture the sleeping house, lights off, the angle of the couch facing the television where we had watched the hearings. I could see the magazines and ashtrays on the end tables, the pillows we rearranged when we kissed while listening to Steely Dan's "Dirty Work."

I stepped back from the door and said, out loud, "Come on, Suzanne."

Then I heard the doorknob rattle and the lock turn.

The door swung open. Her father stood there. He was wearing flannel pajamas and a robe, no glasses. He had an unlit filter cigarette stuck in the corner of his mouth.

He nodded hello. "She asked me to give you this."

He handed me a white business envelope. It was sealed and heavy. I must have looked confused.

"It's from Suzanne," he said.

"I know," I said. "We were supposed to have breakfast."

"You were," he said. "She's not coming down."

He shrugged, pulled the cigarette out of his mouth, and examined it. He coughed a gooey cough and started pushing the door closed. Then he pointed at the envelope. "She said read it. You'll understand." The door clicked shut and the lock turned.

I stood there a second and then got back in my car. I remember I slammed the car door hard. For some reason, I raised the envelope to my face and smelled it. The paper felt cool against my lips. It smelled like mint.

Inside the envelope there were four or five pieces of paper. On top was a handwritten note. She said she was sorry. She said she was engaged to be married. The engagement had just happened. Long-term boyfriend, out of her life, then suddenly back in it.

Johnny.

At the end, she signed off. Not sincerely, not warmly. Not with regret. Not even her full name. Just the initial, *S*.

Along with the note she had enclosed three or four poems. She had typed them for me, each one perfectly framed on its page. I sat in the driveway and read the one on top by Kahlil Gibran. I learned that there were spaces in our togetherness, that the strings of the lute were alone and quivering, that the oak tree and the cypress could not grow in each other's shadow. This message was very helpful. It was a sigh to let me go by. I imagined Suzanne rolling sheets of paper into her typewriter, opening a book, and meticulously typing those poems. Or maybe she had memorized them.

The truth is, I was sort of relieved. I had flunked the test. I felt lucky. I folded up the papers and put them back in the envelope. And I remembered: breakfast.

The hostess at Lil Chef told me I could sit anywhere. When I asked her if Delphine was working that morning, she nodded and pointed. I took a booth in her section, next to a window that looked out on the road. Across the street was a department store parking lot, more or less empty on Sunday morning. Gulls whirled above it, landed, and strutted around puddles. Delphine brought me eggs and potatoes and coffee. She had nice nails and long fingers and long artificially black hair gathered in a ponytail she wore over her right shoulder. She called me "Hon."

She was refilling my coffee cup when I said to her, "I thought you were sick."

She set my bill on the table and cocked her head. "What?"

I told her I knew Suzanne. "She said you were sick. She was covering a couple shifts for you. Last night. And Friday night."

"She did, that's right."

"She did?" I said. "Really?" That much, at least, was true.

"She's a sweet kid. And smart."

I didn't know about sweet. I said, yes, she certainly was smart.

"She wants to be a lawyer."

"That's what I hear," I said.

"I could see her doing that," Delphine said. She gave the coffee-pot a gentle shake. "I just hope she doesn't get stuck doing this." She thought for a minute and then added, "It's easy for a girl to get stuck."

I took a while finishing my coffee. There was a newspaper on the table with fresh Watergate news—the tapes, the special prosecutor, the obstruction of justice charges. Could Nixon survive? What did the President know, and when did he know it? The questions seemed simple enough where impeachable offenses were concerned. But between two people, maybe not. What did we know, and when did we know it?

I left Delphine a nice tip from my Red Fox money and waved goodbye to her on the way out. I had a two-hour drive back to school on not quite enough sleep. I had AM radio to keep me company. At the end of the term, I would have to get my car fixed. That was six weeks and a couple more psych tests away.

11

Love at First Shite

I've had sewage on my mind since watching the Coen brothers' *True Grit*. Early in the movie, Mattie Ross's search for Rooster Cogburn leads her to an outhouse. When she knocks on the door, we hear Jeff Bridges's Rooster growl from inside: "The jakes is occupied." Mattie knocks again, and Rooster says again, with even more gravel, "I said the jakes is occupied."

"The jakes" is a term I remember from my Shakespeare. And here it is, in a Hollywood movie. There is so much linguistic weirdness in *True Grit*. (The lingo they use. And where'd the contractions go?) This opening scene, for me, is love at first shite.

But then I started wondering: Would Rooster Cogburn have used the word "jakes"? Instead of outhouse, let's say, or crapper, crib, earth closet, hutch, john, latrine, privy, shitter, or tollhouse? It got me thinking too about how pungent life must have been—especially city life—in Rooster Cogburn's time and in most of history before his time.

I have been acquainted with the jakes. My paternal grandparents lived on a farm with no indoor plumbing. The outhouse sat at the edge of the backyard, a few feet from the corn crib and across the drive from the barn, where cows often did their business while being milked. (The outhouse smelled much worse than the barn.) Against my will, when nature called I used the outhouse, pulling the door shut, looking down through that zero on the seat as if into a smelly abyss. When I spent the night, my grandmother pulled a chamber pot from under the bed and invited me to make water. The performance anxiety was unbearable. I was so modern and yet so Puritanical in my upbringing that I could barely bring myself to say the word "toilet." And I had to tinkle in that thing?

Then there were the outdoor toilets at the campgrounds where our parents took us for vacation. In a stroke of genius someone in the state of Michigan had decided that a good color for the toilets was brown. In some of the forest camps, there was a cement slab, walls, stalls, cans, no water, and very bad smells that were vented into the external air. (I'm convinced these vents were merely ornamental.) At the more primitive campgrounds, there were even more dreadful offices.

One of my most vivid memories of the jakes is from my college days. After tramping out to the shitter at Denny Vickroy's cottage in West Branch one subzero morning, I sat on a very frosty seat and worried my ass would freeze to it.

The outhouse was where man met beast, and the beast was himself.

The Romans, true to form, were on top of things. The Cloaca Maxima, a giant civil sewage system, went online around 600 BC. Initially an open-air canal (essentially a ditch) during Etruscan times, it was covered by the Romans, which must have contained the stench. The Cloaca Maxima conveyed rainwater and runoff—along with chamber potage—to the Tiber. Then came aqueducts, eleven of them, that brought fresh water to the city. By 100 AD, there were latrines in some homes, some with running water (recycled from the public baths). In 315 AD, the city had 140 public latrines. These were sanitary people.

It would seem the latrine (from the Latin *lavatrina*, meaning "a place to wash") was a social place. Romans who gathered there to make deposits also exchanged gossip and talked politics. Sewage literature also speaks of an object, almost too revolting for words, called a "communal sponge" in the Roman latrine. These were sanitary people? The loo (from "Room 100" or "Waterloo"?) continues to be a social place. Ladies like to go together. My wife recalls coming to Freeland for the first time, for a romp at the Rathole bar, and overhearing a girl in the john. "She was going on and on about beer piss," she told me. Then she quoted: "'I try to delay going as long as I can. Sometimes I'll wait for hours. Because once you start, you'll be pissing all night.'" It was common knowledge among my friends, but to my wife, not a beer drinker, this was a rustic tidbit.

We turned together and looked at the dance floor.

"Her," she said.

Wild hair. A rhythmic, flopping dance. It was Bonny. I knew she knew her piss.

The summer before, she and I had occasionally taken long drives together with six-packs of beer. We had long conversations about friends, about life, driving twenty-five miles per hour past farms and fields. At length, one of us would have to go. I'd pull over, stand at the edge of the road, and relieve myself in the direction of the ditch, watching the cattails sway in the moonlight. When I'd finished, while I waited in the car, Bonny would get out and sit on the bumper of my vw and do her business. I have to say, I loved her for that. It wasn't enough to base a relationship on. But almost.

I thought "the jakes" must be in, around, and all over Shakespeare's corpus. It's not. The term appears only once, in *King Lear*.

Thou whoreson zed! thou unnecessary letter! My
lord, if you will give me leave, I will tread this

unbolted villain into mortar, and daub the wall of
   a jakes with him.

Daub the walls, fill the cracks, keep the wind out, keep the bad air in. So it's not all over Shakespeare, but "jakes" appears to have been a popular slang word for the outhouse during his time. The *Oxford English Dictionary*'s first example of its use dates 1438. My old *Webster's* simply labels it archaic.

I am happy to have found a lengthy disquisition on sewage in Elizabethan times, John Harington's *A New Discourse of a Stale Subject, called The Metamorphosis of Ajax* ("Ajax" being a play on "a jakes"). Harington is the inventor of the flush toilet. He is the John who gives his name to, and is honored by, our visits to the john. Gail Kern Paster, Director of the Folger Shakespeare Library, sees in Harington's work—his discourse, and I guess his toilet too—an "elaborate attempt to reconstruct his audience's orientation to dung and excretion in general." In her scholarly reading of Harington, Dolly Jørgensen, professor of ecology and environmental science at the University of Sweden, notes with appreciation that Harington "understands filth from privies as a particularly urban phenomenon and one with health consequences." No one can say it quite like Harington:

> when companies of men began first to increase, and make of families townes, and of townes cities; they quickly found not onely offence, but infection, to grow out of great concourse of people, if speciall care were not had to avoyd it. And because they could not remove houses, as they do tents, from place to place, they were driven to find the best meanes that their wits did then serve them, to cover, rather then to avoyd these annoyances: either by digging pits in the earth, or placing the common houses over rivers . . .

Fast forward to the privy in the backyard, to the frosty jakes behind Denny Vickroy's cottage. The problem was and is always the same: what to do with poo.

Some time after we were married, my wife and I camped at one of those campgrounds. Make that "camped." We stayed in my parents' house trailer, a Hilton on Higgins Lake. One night before turning off the light, I suggested we walk to the restroom. She said no.

"I'm using the bathroom in the trailer," she said. This made sense. It was a space smaller than a phone booth, but it was clean and odor free. On the other hand, our using the Hilton head meant my father would have to transfer, by way of pump, our "black water" to a pit in the earth near the camp exit. I thought we could save him the trouble.

"Why don't we just walk over there," I said.

"No."

"It's totally modern now." Concrete floors. A strong antiseptic smell. The detritus of many, many users. "They're nice."

"You go."

There was no persuading her. I knew that. "Okay," I said. "I will."

I stepped out of the trailer and shut the door. It was a cold, moonless night. I should have waited a minute for my eyes to adjust to the dark, but I didn't. Instead I stepped off purposefully in the direction of the new and improved jakes and walked right into a tree.

In Harington's time, in keeping with miasma theory, people believed disease was transmitted through bad smells and stench. As Harington writes, "they quickly found not onely offence, but infection, to grow out of great concourse of people." I don't know if Harington's invention prevented a single case of bubonic plague, but I'm quite sure it prevented a great many people from walking into trees.

Would Rooster have called the privy "the jakes"? I'm beginning to doubt the term had wide use among speakers of English in west

Arkansas in the 1870s. Maybe it was a term Rooster's father or mother used, and he affectionately clung to it.

I stood in the library and took down regional dictionaries and tried to learn the truth. The more I read, the more I thought about my orientation to dung and excrement. Jørgensen's treatment of *The Metamorphosis of Ajax* suggests there's a deep literature to wade through. She writes, "In spite of anthropological literature such as Elias' *Civilizing Process*, Duby's *A History of Private Life*, and Laporte's *History of Shit* that stress the late medieval development of privacy and shame associated with biological functions, privies as property were very much a public matter." These must be tomes, heavy reading not available in paperback. Something you take with you to the jakes.

12

Feet First

We're in the balcony of the theater in Stratford. It's May 1974. I'm twenty-one years old, visiting England for cultural enrichment. This trip should be heaven—it is mostly heaven—but it also includes a production of *King John*. Even Shakespeare, I've learned, could have an off day. During intermission, the lights are up, and I'm sitting next to my new friend Michelle, who I am about to discover has a phobia. Behind her, an oaf in our group named Barton exhales a huge yawn, stretches himself, and lays a foot in the gap between our seats. It's a big foot, out of its shoe, out of its sock, and even to me it's as shocking and grotesque as a cold, dead fish. But to Michelle the foot is evil. She shrieks. Fortunately we're a few rows back from the rail of the balcony. Otherwise I have no doubt she would swan dive to escape the obscenity of that foot.

Many years later, visiting my parents, I remember Michelle's hysterical reaction. My mother is already well into dementia. My father, eighty-eight years old, is mentally razor sharp and still physically strong. Except, these days, for his leg. I'm here to look at the leg. I've invited myself to lunch, which he prepares, limping from the kitchen to the dining room table to lay out soup, lunch meats, bread, cottage cheese, and mixed fruit.

"We're doing okay," he says. A cane leans against his chair in the living room. He's determined to take care of my mother, to keep her out of assisted living as long as possible, even to the end, even if it kills him.

"Have you had it looked at?"

"I took some aspirin last night," he says. He carries water glasses to the table. "That helped some."

My mother comes to the table and sits down. She's been looking for some girls in the other room, some girls that exist only in her mind. She smiles at me—a conspiratorial smile that suggests we're sharing a little joke. When my dad sits down we say grace and eat. Throughout the meal, he reminds her of her business. *Finish your soup. That's your bread. Would you like some more cheese?*

We save the leg for dessert.

And it's a doozy. After lunch, he pulls up his pant leg and shows me his swollen limb. It's the color of a rotting plum. At the end of the leg, looking like it could explode any minute, is my father's foot.

As body parts go, the foot doesn't get much respect. We lavish care upon hair, call eyes the windows of the soul, and look with awe upon skilled hands. Breasts, legs, and even butts are the objects of desire, the stuff of fetish. Feet, also fetish-worthy, get some attention. On the other hand, with their thick slabs of scaly calluses, their hideous toenails so like hooves and horns, feet link us to the animal world. Feet remind us we are of the earth. Humble feet take us on this journey through life. We owe them greatly, yet we look upon them only when we have to.

There are feet, one might say, and there are feet. In Quentin Tarantino's *Pulp Fiction*, John Travolta and Samuel L. Jackson stand with their backs to the camera, discoursing about the degree of intimacy and the erotic import of foot massage. If you take the time to look, you might see that Uma Thurman has a fine foot. "They flee from me," Sir Thomas Wyatt wrote, "that sometime did me seek / With naked foot, stalking in my chamber."

I have a friend who wears a tiny gold ring on one toe. In flip-flops, she has a comely enough foot, but in the end, it's still just a foot. I have never heard anyone rhapsodize about feet. In high school, a kid I knew always said, "I like a girl with nice teeth." Not feet. Teeth. Like many people, I'm blessed with moderately prehensile toes. But is that a blessing? At a picnic, I can pick up a fallen napkin with a bare foot. But who would then dab their lips with that napkin?

When my kids were infants I often put their bare feet in my mouth. About the time they started walking, I stopped.

Some years ago I accompanied my son to a birthday party. He was in elementary school. The party was on a winter weeknight, at a roller skating rink. We drove through ice and slush, arriving a little late, and once inside we were greeted, as always, by the unmistakable, pervasive smell of feet. While my son skated with his friends, I sat with moms and dads. One dad was a podiatrist. He was a cheerful, nervous man who worked hard and planned, he said, to retire at fifty.

That night when it came time for pizza and cake, the skating area cleared. I tied on rented skates and started doing laps, enjoying the exhilaration of having wheels fixed to my feet, enjoying the music, the speed on the straightaways, the centrifugal thrill of counter-clockwise curves. On one of these curves—why I don't know—one skate betrayed me, and I went down, hard.

You know when your bones break. I knew. I felt a quick, hot pain and broke into a cold sweat. Mostly, I noticed a sudden loss of function in my left hand. I rolled off the floor—can you limp on skates?—toward pizza and cake.

"I saw that," the podiatrist said. He sat me down. He took my hand in his, gently palpated the area. He put my arm in a sling and iced the wrist. He laid an ice pack on the back of my neck and told me the name of a wrist man to ask for at the hospital. I remember leaving the rink and its footy smell that night, gaining the cold fresh air. Someone drove me to emergency.

I never again put wheels between my feet and the ground.

My father has a long episode. Infection, antibiotics, swelling, and a tender, terrifying foot. Then he recovers. He gets back on his feet. He takes care of my mother. He walks up and down the stairs of their home. He takes my mother to the grocery store, where they slowly make their way up and down aisles. He drives to the podiatrist.

The podiatrist who held my hand gave up feet and retired some time ago. After England, Michelle walked in her Earth shoes out of my life and never came back. How many pairs of shoes have I worn out since then? The feet go on. Poor, underappreciated feet. They are puffy and irresistible as dinner rolls on babies. Bulbous with bunions and corns, they are fungus farms on the aged. Feet are gross and great.

When we approach the edge of the water, it's a lowly toe that goes first. We await its verdict. It's all right. We can go.

13

For Donna, Ibsen, Pepys, Levitation

She follows me back to my office. Her name is Donna.

She wears jeans like all the other girls. Only hers are the baggy kind, the comfortable fit for a woman in her thirties. She sits in the front row, one leg crossed over the other. It bounces, this leg, like she's a piece of machinery that's idling. It's the sixth week of class, and I know this about her: She hasn't been to college in fourteen years. She has two boys. She has a husband whom she has left but who refuses to leave her. Whatever we read in class she reads as if her life depended on it. This week it's Ibsen. To most students, reading *Ghosts* is like swallowing a horse tranquilizer. To Donna, the play is like liquid light, and she chugs it. Sitting there in class, two students over from my desk, she is a presence.

I unlock my office door and let myself in. "What's up?" I say, dropping my books on the desk.

"I just wanted to tell you I may have to miss class." She leans against the door frame and tells me what I was afraid to hear. It's him. He's hanging around. She's afraid he's going to take her kids. She's afraid.

"It shouldn't be a problem," I say, "if you have to miss." I tell her I can work with her.

"It's just that I'm enjoying this so much."

I tell her we're glad to have her in class.

"That Pastor Manders," she says, referring to the Ibsen. "When he tells Mrs. Alving: 'We're not put on this earth to be happy.' How can he say that to her?" She shakes her head. "Those people are so miserable."

"Just wait," I say.

She laughs. "I saw *Ghosts* on the syllabus, you know what I thought of?"

It's my turn to laugh. "Patrick Swayze?"

"In school, like in ninth grade, we did this thing called levitation." She gives me an embarrassed look. "Did you ever levitate?"

Did I ever.

My first time was tenth grade. I was at Sandra Bremer's house. I guess it was a party, boys and girls together on a Saturday night, not couples, just six or seven unattached kids together, and someone said we should play "Let's pick him up."

"You lie on the floor," Sandra said, "and everyone gathers around the person. You say these words together, and then, using just your fingertips, you can pick the person up."

We moved furniture out of the way. Someone shut the lights off. Then we took turns volunteering to lie on the floor in the living room, pretending we were dead, while the others gathered around, looking down at the dark form on the floor. The ceremony was very solemn.

The first person said, "He is dead." One after another, going around the circle, we took turns repeating that line and those that followed.

Gone from the earth.
Stiff as a board.
Light as a feather.

At this point we bent down and slipped two fingers of each hand under the person's body. The leader said, "Let's pick him up." And we did.

It worked every time. The dead person, no matter how big, would practically fly up to the ceiling, where we held him for a split second before lowering him back down to the floor. We would gasp and scream for a minute or two, terrified and amazed by this mystery in the dark, and then ask for another volunteer. No one tried to understand what was happening. We didn't want to understand it. It was pure joy. It was like direct contact with the supernatural.

When there were no more volunteers, we switched the lights back on, put the furniture back in place, and turned on Cat Stevens. If there was a scary movie on TV, we'd watch that.

There's a reference to levitation as a party trick in *The Magician's Own Book, or the Whole Art of Conjuring* by George Arnold and Frank Cahill, published in 1862. The authors describe it as "one of the most remarkable and inexplicable experiments relative to the strength of the human frame." In their description, they emphasize that it is a "heavy man" who is lifted when his lungs and the lungs of those lifting are fully inflated with air. The authors trace this magic back to an American navy captain doing a demonstration in Venice. The critical detail, according to Arnold and Cahill, is the breathing: "On several occasions [we] have observed that when one of the bearers performs his part ill, by making the inhalation out of time, the part of the body which he tries to raise is left, as it were, behind."

Two centuries earlier, Samuel Pepys refers to levitation in his diary entry on July 31, 1665. He provides an account of leaving London to attend a wedding, noting in that week alone, some seventeen or eighteen hundred people had died of plague (one-tenth of the London population died that year). Pepys and his party arrive too late for the ceremony but in time for dinner, cards, talk, and prayers. After helping put the newlyweds to bed ("I kissed the bride in bed, and so the curtaines drawne with the greatest gravity that could be, and so good night"), he goes to a bed which, consistent with customs of the time, he shares with another guest.

Before sleep, the two men have a chat. "We did here all get good beds, and I lay in the same I did before with Mr. Brisband, who is a good scholler and sober man; and we lay in bed, getting him to give me an account of home, which is the most delightfull talke a man can have of any traveller." In the course of their conversation, Mr. Brisband speaks of "enchantments and spells" he has recently witnessed in Bourdeaux, France. "He saw four little girles," Pepys writes, "very young ones, all kneeling, each of them, upon one knee; and one begun the first line, whispering in the eare of the next, and the second to the third, and the third to the fourth, and she to the first." They whisper these words:

Voyci un Corps mort (Behold, a dead body),
Royde comme un Baston (Still as a stone),
Froid comme Marbre (Cold as marble),
Leger comme un esprit (Light as a spirit),
Levons te au nom de Jesus Christ (We lift you in the
    name of Jesus Christ).

With one finger each, they raise the boy as high as they can reach. Brisband is "afeard to see it" and—disbelieving—calls for the cook, "a very lusty fellow," meaning large, to come, and in like manner, the girls lift him as well.

For a while, every time that group of friends got together, at Sandra Bremer's or wherever, we shut off the lights and played dead, picking each other up. We reveled in the mystery of levitation. Like those little French girls, what we were enjoying was essentially child's play, like telling ghost stories, though in our case, we didn't have bubonic plague adding spice to the experience. Looking back now, I marvel at the fact that we never dropped anyone. What were the chances? But no one banged his head on an end table. No one fell and broke an arm.

My preferred role in the game was the dead guy. Lying on the floor, eyes closed, listening to the chant—to feel myself lifted into the air was a rush, not so much an out-of-body as an in-body experience. Some nights, along with levitation, there was talk of séances and hypnosis. I remember seeing kids bent over a Ouija board. "Wouldn't it be freaky," someone said, "to see into the future?"

Sure, but what if you had to see all of it?

If there's any wisdom in becoming an adult, it's knowing that you don't want to know. We grow up. We marry and have children. We divorce and find ourselves alone again. In search of ourselves we fly off to faraway places and then come back home, still searching. Our parents, spouses, and friends, sometimes even our children, sicken and die. Between these events, there are the levitations, moments of genuine sweetness and mystery you share with other people. Lying in bed with Mr. Brisband, Pepys observes, "I have spent the greatest part of my life with abundance of joy, and honour, and pleasant journeys, and brave entertainments," calling the wedding and his time with friends the "greatest glut of content that ever [he] had; only under some difficulty because of the plague."

Seeing Donna in class, reading and thinking and sharing, was like witnessing a levitation.

A week passed before I heard from her. She called me to apologize for being absent. She was in a shelter. She said she couldn't talk long. She said he didn't know where she was and that her safety, and the safety of her children, depended on keeping her whereabouts a secret. I told her to take care of herself, that we were just finishing

Ghosts, and that she could come back anytime and write the paper, pick up where she left off.

When we hung up, I had an idea she wouldn't be back. A week passed, then another. In class we moved along to the next works on the syllabus—*The Crucible*, *Wise Blood*, *Go Tell It on the Mountain*—works Donna would have loved. I never saw her again.

14

The Soft Imperative

I ask my wife, "What language do they speak in Macedonia?"
It's a Friday morning. This is our pre-breakfast quiet time. Usually
we don't say much early in the morning. What is there to always
say? She's reading a book about the Spanish Civil War and drinking
her first cup of coffee. I've just clicked off the *New Yorker*, which I'm
partially reading online these days. Anthony Lane has yawned at
Black Mass, the new Johnny Depp movie, comparing it and Depp
unfavorably to *Taxi!* and James Cagney. I'm about to spread fig
jam on a slice of toast.

She turns a page. "Macedonian? Or maybe Greek." She looks
up. "You really should read this book. You never read the books I
suggest."

"I read *The Swerve*," I say. "I started to read *The Skin*."

"Started."

It's a new jar of jam. The jar pops when I twist the cap off. "Brian's
Fig Marmalade," I read aloud. "From Macedonia. You wouldn't
think there would be a guy named Brian in Macedonia."

She picks up the jar, squints at the fine print, and hands it back.

Between slices of toast, I borrow her iPad. "You're right, Macedonian. It says the Macedonians are slavophones."

She nods.

"Slavophones," I say, waiting for her to make eye contact. "I would hate to be called a slavophone." Another pregnant pause. "How about you?"

She taps her spoon against her cup. It's code: more coffee. I've told her she should just say, "Coffee me!" when she wants more, the way guys back in my college days would shout, "Beer me!" That was fun. Verbing the noun added to the casual derangement you felt on a beerful afternoon.

I make her a second cappuccino. This morning, thanks to "coffee me," which my wife refuses to say, and thanks to Mount Everest and the *New Yorker*, I'm thinking about verbs. Anthony Lane also reviewed the new movie *Everest*. Too many characters, he writes, most of them underdeveloped. "The one thing they have in common," he observes, "is the indomitable urge to use the word 'summit' as an intransitive verb. That takes guts."

"Here you go." I set her coffee down, admiring the foam. "Enjoy."

"You know I hate that."

I know she hates it, that universal server-ism you hear in restaurants these days. The plates are all delivered, the wine glasses filled, we're ready to eat, and the server says, "Enjoy." Not "Enjoy your dinner." Not "Enjoy yourselves." Just "Enjoy." The locution irks her no end.

It irks me too, but not no end.

Later in the day I'm driving over to the blood depot, a couple of miles from the house. Every eight weeks I shed a pint. I do it both for the common good and for my personal benefit. (Back in college, the old beer-me days, I learned to call this psychological egoism. There's no such thing as a selfless act. You beered your friends knowing they would beer you back. It was a social contract.) According to the *American Journal of Epidemiology*, blood donors are 88 percent less likely to suffer heart attack. Old blood has higher viscosity than the new stuff you make. So bleed me. I'm happy to give.

On the drive over there, I stop at a light behind a car with a personalized license plate: "Be Well." The phrase reminds me of an old friend, David Marvin Cooper, a laid-back guy who always used to say, "Be cool." He meant go with the flow, be open to the universe, or sometimes, a little more sternly, don't be bogue (dude). "Be well" says much the same thing, maybe more. Roll down your window and smell the roses. Dial down the Rush Limbaugh and turn up the Mozart. Accept road work as a part of life. It's a philosophical concept. It gentles us, reminding strangers to be mindful. This driver is concerned, in his or her generalized and impersonal way, with way more than my well-being or my wellness.

A physician I saw for a short time, whenever I left her office, would touch me on the shoulder and say: "Feel better." She also said apply ice, take your pain meds, no stairs. But then she capped it off with a holistic prescription that went beyond mere better-getting.

These are the soft state-of-being imperatives available to us today, helping us to be well and good.

The blood center is packed. I've made an appointment, but I still have to wait. I pretend to read the Red Cross book for a few minutes, picking out some diseases I might want to check up on (babesiosis, filariasis, spondylosis), and then look at old news in used magazines, too many of which are about golf. During the interview and Q and A, the nurse takes my temperature and blood pressure, examines my arms. She asks me if I had a good breakfast, if I've had plenty of liquids. I tell her about Brian's Fig Marmalade, trying to remember as I do if Macedonia is on the list of places the Red Cross has associated with disease and dubious blood.

"Right or left?" she asks, meaning, *Which arm?*

I tell her I'm left leaning. For me, it's part of being well.

On the table, I make a fist. She inflates the blood pressure cuff and says I have nice veins. When the bleeding starts, she eases the cuff. I relax and roll the thingie in my hand. I watch local news on TV and try to dislodge a few fig seeds from my teeth. At one time, giving blood made me light-headed. Donating at work one day, I sat up too fast and felt a radical wobble in my legs. A blue shirt sat me back down and made me put my head between my knees. Another time I got the paper bag treatment. That was then. These days I'm manning up. I can give and give.

The nurse comes by again to check on me and my bag of blood. "Almost done," she says. "You doing okay?"

I tell her I'm good. And well as well.

Wrapping my arm when it's finished, she points to the juice and cookie table. "No strenuous activity today," she says. "Watch a little TV. Do a little reading."

On the way home I see the usual guy on the usual corner, holding a cardboard sign. In black felt pen he has written "PLEASE HELP." Word has it there's a meth ring in town, and this guy might be an affiliate. Wouldn't you know it, I come to a full stop right next to him. "Look at their teeth," I've been told. But I can't. I just sit. Between me and him, a few feet, a universe. Somewhere in between the two categoricals—Get a job! Feed the poor!—is the soft imperative, an intransitive zone. Be well. Out of the corner of my eye, I see him wave his little sign. There's no telling what help is, what's good for both of us.

The light changes.

Go.

15

Third-Wave Coffee

Next to me at the counter, this girl and her phone are having a sandwich. The sandwich is made with thick artisanal bread. I see tomato, sprouts, and white goo that, if she's not careful, might *splop* on her phone, which is strategically positioned between her plate and her coffee cup. When the phone lights up every minute or so, she left-hands the sandwich, smiles down at the screen, and taps it with her right forefinger. She takes a sip of coffee.

Me too. I'm here for some coffee.

I mean Coffee.

It's my fourth visit to this coffee bar, Astro, on Michigan Avenue, down the street from what's left of Detroit's train station, up the street from the vacant lot that was Tiger Stadium. Astro is in Corktown, one of those places that's happening in Detroit. It's old made new, it's Detroit waking up. At Astro you can get a tight espresso, a perfect macchiato, and a respectable cappuccino. They also serve pour-overs made from the coffees listed on the board behind the bar. Today they're pour-overing Montecarlos (El Salvador), El Prado (Columbia), La Folie (Guatemala), Karinga (Kenya), and Chorongi (Kenya).

According to 2010 Census data, the average Detroiter (a person sixteen years or older living in the city limits) travels twenty-six miles to get to work. How far does a Detroiter have to travel to get a good cup of coffee? Of course there's coffee just about everywhere, and by coffee I mean the thin, steaming swill you get at lunch stands, breakfast shacks, convenience stores, and gas stations. Want that to go? Our Styrofoam cups come in two sizes.

But what about Coffee? I checked. Inside the Detroit city limits, 138 square miles, there are tentatively four Starbucks. When I Google "a good espresso in Detroit," a foursquare.com link takes me to "The 13 Best Places for Espresso in Detroit." At that page I find the headline has been downgraded to "The 9 Best Places for Espresso in Detroit" (hence "tentatively" above). Another link lists forty-three spots, a few of which I'd certainly try, just because I like their names: Tongues Coffee, Café 1923, Zanie Janie, Ugly Mug. Most of these places are not in Detroit (Wyandotte, Ferndale, Northville, Plymouth, Brighton, Ypsilanti). I like the sound of Conga Coffee until I see this: Mount Clemens. And this: "Now features an Acoustic Guitar Circle for Adult Beginners."

And many of these forty-three are arguably not legitimate Coffee contenders because they are chains—Biggby, Caribou, Coffee Beanery, Panera, and, alas, Starbucks. These are PC (paper cup) second-wave providers.

Coffee—and I mean Coffee in its espresso incarnation, first-wave Coffee—begins in Italy, in 1901, when Luigi Bezzera invents an apparatus, essentially a boiler, that forces (expresses) hot water through compressed coffee. The machine makes it possible to produce individual servings of coffee in forty-five seconds, "expressly" for each individual. In 1947, Achille Gaggia refines the technology and process, activating, as Jonathon Morris reports, "essential oils and colloids from the coffee, creating a mousse or crema on top of the resultant beverage." First-wave espresso came to the United States in 1921 (Tosca Caffe, San Francisco) or maybe it was 1927 (Caffe Reggio, New York); first cappuccino came in 1957 (Caffe Trieste, San Francisco).

Years later came PC second-wave coffee. Only it wasn't a wave. It was a tsunami. Suddenly it became common to see people taking their Grande, "small" in PC speak, for a walk down the street or driving down the road holding a Venti, the twenty-ounce container, probably with stuff in the coffee. A lot of stuff. Suddenly sentences such as these, heretofore unimaginable in English, became common:

I'll have Tazo berry with cream, plus a shot of mocha.

I'd like an iced mocha cappuccino with an extra shot of chocolate, skim milk, decaf. I can't stand the taste of coffee . . . it has to taste like hot cocoa instead.

I'm in the mood for a tall nonfat caramel and honey half-decaf/half-regular latte with a little whipped cream on top.

Frappuccino.

Some of this stuff you can't even say in Italian.

We're well into the third wave now. Independent providers like Astro, for whom coffee is a business but also very much an art, science, and religion, are coming on strong, growing by 20 percent a year, making up 8 percent of the yearly $18 billion coffee market. We can be thankful.

We can be thankful, for example, for real ceramic cups. Drinking espresso, or worse, cappuccino from a paper cup is like eating steak with a spork. Give me a cup, with a handle, with a saucer, with a miniature spoon. At independents they grind (Astro calls it "shredding"), they weigh coffee shots (an Astro shot weighs a whopping nineteen grams), they monitor water temperature (around two hundred degrees Fahrenheit), they warm the cups. When the independents do it right, they serve a Coffee so dense, with a crema so thick, you can almost spread it on toast.

Astro does it right.

One Saturday morning my wife and I order coffee at Astro. Her cappuccino comes with a Christmas tree in the foam.

I point at the sign. "Miranda, from Columbia," I say to the barista. "Is that your usual espresso?"

She says no, the coffees come in twenty-pound bags. When Miranda's gone, they'll rotate. She hands me my macchiato. There's a heart in the foam.

"So if we come back next week, or the week after?"

"It probably won't be Miranda," she says.

Hmm.

Ten days later, I'm back. She's right. They're shredding Owl's Howl. And it tastes . . . different.

Around the corner from where my niece lives and works in Pesaro, Italy, is a Pascucci coffee bar. Pascucci is a brand, a roaster, a franchise. Kind of like Starbucks. Only different. "Ricky," she says one day, "you have to try it." I do. And I say it's great. When I'm back in town a year later, I try it again. Still great. More to the point: same great. Up the coast, in Santarcangelo di Romagna, my wife and I find a Pascucci bar. It's a sunny day. We sit outside under an awning, at the edge of the big piazza, and have coffee. My espresso, great. Her macchiato, great.

It turns out the Pascucci coffee bean works, the *torrefazione*, is located just a few miles from both Pesaro and Santarcangelo. It's also just fifteen to twenty miles from our apartment in San Marino. I might say to cousins or friends, "Hey, one day, why don't we drive over to Monte Cerignone and check out Pascucci? You know, have a cup of coffee?" I might say that, and I know what the response would be.

No.

Along with Pascucci, there's another coffee outfit right in Pesaro, called Foschi. I might ask cousins and friends: "Have you ever been there?"

No.

Part of this is temperament. An American will drive a long distance to go to the source. This explains the American winehead's willingness to make the very long, albeit scenic, trek to Montalcino to drink wine he buys down the street at home. Part of it is just an Italian's sense of the old normal. There's good wine everywhere. The Pascucci bar is a two-minute walk. You go to Pascucci or Foschi or Saccaria or Segafredo or Caffè Nero, all of them roasters, all of them franchises, and every time you go, the coffee tastes good.

I'd say great. A great that is normal.

A few years ago I had dinner with a plumber in Tuscany, at the edge of Chianti country. We started the meal with a cheese plate. On the plate were slices of sheep's milk cheese, pecorino fresco. It's a soft, mild cheese. You might daub a little honey on it or just have it plain.

"There's nothing like this in the states," I said.

"It's good," he said.

I took a bite and smiled. "It's great," I said.

He shook his head and pointed to the road we had driven to get to the restaurant. When he was a kid, he said, up that road, next to his house was a farmer who had three sheep. They grazed on a hillside behind the farmer's house. Every year the farmer made the pecorino from those sheep's milk. He held up a slice of cheese and examined it. "This is good, but it's not great. It's hard to get great anymore."

In 2008, the producers of Parmigiano-Reggiano formed a consortium to guarantee quality of the Parmigiano cheese. (Mario Batali always refers to it as "the king of cheeses.")

These organizations are called DOCs: *Denominazione di origine controllata*, a label you also see on some Italian wine. The consortium regulates ingredients, production, and aging. Cheeses that conform can claim the name Parmigiano-Reggiano.

Some time ago I was reading about the DOC's impact on the cheese. The cheese is good, the food writer said, it's very good (I'd say it's great), but there are no longer those surprise cheeses, the ones that come along every five to ten years, mind-blowing cheeses, for example, that taste of fall or spring. You just get good cheese.

In this case, I'll take good. Pecorino fresco, Parmigiano-Reggiano, Pascucci espresso. Good every time. I'd say they're great.

Italians stand and slam an espresso. They may look at a newspaper for a minute and exchange a few words with the barista or patrons. But the coffee? They drink it hot and fast, and then they go. The bars they frequent are down the street from their house or workplace. Americans are more inclined to taste, to *experience* the coffee, finding fruits, textures, complexities. Here's the Owl's Howl roaster description of that coffee: "This blend displays a deep, honey-like body, with notes of ripe berry, chocolate-covered cherry, and sweet candied lemon." This is coffee you study.

Giorgio Milos, a master barista for Illy brand coffee in Trieste, drank espresso all over New York a few years ago, trying to gauge similarities and differences in the coffee. "Americans," he observes in *Salon*, "are creating their own traditions, such as making espresso with single-origin beans—i.e. beans that come from one farm or estate, to highlight the characteristics of that place—while Italian espresso is made from blends that often include some lesser-quality—i.e. Robusta—beans. In Illy's blend there are no fewer than nine bean types."

Third-wave is our wave, and this is not your father's caffe americano. The standard weight of an espresso shot in Italy is seven to eight-and-a-half grams. Astro is pressing and expressing nineteen grams. I'm not sure what they're up to. It's a bomb blast. Whatever they're up to, it's a step in the right direction. I'll drive all the way to Astro for a Detroit coffee bar experience, fifteen minutes from work, thirty minutes from home. I'll take my time and try to learn about flavor profiles. I'll sip and dream of Italy, happy to be in Detroit.

16

Wisdom Teeth and
Encyclopaedia Britannica

He says he'd like to keep his teeth. It's no surprise. They'll be a curiosity to photograph and display to friends on Facebook. Then they'll probably end up on a shelf, little remarked upon, collecting dust.

Right now, minus two wisdom teeth, my son is propped up by a couple of pillows on the couch. He holds a pink plastic dish to his face and drools a gooey pink mix of saliva and blood into it.

"How do you feel?" I say.

He gives me a nod, his chipmunk cheeks distended by gauze pads putting pressure on the vacancies.

"In a few hours," I tell him, "you can have a pain med." Then an hour later, the nurse said, a couple of Tylenol. Or was it Motrin? I can't remember. "Don't spit," I remind him.

On the way to the oral surgeon that morning, we discussed different kinds of patients, those who disappear into a dark room and want to be left alone (his sister and I), and those who prefer to suffer demonstratively on the couch and want to be taken care of (he and his mother). He gave me a list of foods and beverages to add to the list of foods and beverages suggested by the nurse. I leave him now, pillowed, his face blackening and bluing, to go get soft provisions, liquids, and narcotics.

I'm just pulling into the pharmacy parking lot when I hear an announcement on the radio: *Encyclopaedia Britannica* is calling it quits.

A set of the *Encyclopaedia Britannica* weighs 129 pounds and costs $1,395. In its heyday, Britannica sold 120,000 sets a year. The shortest entry was logged in 1771: "Woman: The female of man."

We had a set when I was a kid, in a custom-built bookcase, on a shelf above the *World Book Encyclopedia*. *World Book*, the spatial arrangement seemed to suggest, was kids' stuff. It was the gateway reference book. You had to work your way up to the *Britannica*.

They might as well have been on the roof. I wasn't going to use them. For one thing, they were so heavy, and the volumes had sharp corners that stabbed your belly and legs. For another, the print was small, the pages were thin, and the language was dense and impenetrable and British. Once or twice I consulted them. I decided I was going to read up on philosophy, but I let that go. Too many pages, too many unpronounceable Greek names, not enough pictures. I read up on the Amazon after I saw *Tarzan and the Amazons* on Saturday morning television and became interested in piranha fish. (*What was Tarzan doing on the Amazon?* I wondered. *And how can there be more than one Amazon?* Questions I did not answer by not reading the *Encyclopaedia Britannica*.) In the interest of self-improvement, I consulted the pages on human reproduction, which *Encyclopaedia Britannica* made about as thrilling as philosophy. Not as many pages (good), unpronounceable Latin names, not enough pictures (bad).

For a parent, it must have been comforting to own the *Encyclopaedia Britannica*. It was like having a piano in the house. There was at least the theoretical possibility of your children improving themselves. An old, out-of-date set of encyclopedias, like a crappy, old piano, could have that effect. Why don't you give a few piano lessons with Mrs. Bell a try? Why don't you read up on electronics?

Out-of-date was no problem, except when the supplements came. Those slender oddball additions Britannica felt obligated to mail out when new knowledge was discovered—who wanted those? They were ugly. They lacked heft. Here we had all the knowledge we would ever need, all red and leather-bound, all gold lettered and alphabetical, and then Britannica sent us those updates.

Encyclopedias prepared you for the real work you would do when you got to school. They were like a life preserver, keeping you afloat before you got to the lifeboat, which I guess was the school library.

Right. When I went to the library, I headed straight for the encyclopedias. Our *World Book* at home had white covers; the ones at school had red. But they smelled the same, and unlike the *Britannica*, whose print was cramped with accuracy and erudition, you could copy from *World Book* without eyestrain.

I don't remember a teacher ever asking me—or anyone, for that matter—did you really write this? Water pollution, here you go. Gettysburg, got that subject covered. Edgar Allen Poe, yeah, I've been reading up on him a lot lately. If I had gone to the library and traced some Monet water lilies for art class and turned them in to Mr. Perry, he would have vivisected me on the spot (he also taught biology). "Do your own work," he would have said. But you could turn in pages and pages of plagiarized writing, and none of those teachers seemed to care.

Looking back, I wish just once I'd copied from the *Britannica*. Maybe that would have rung their bell, violating a code of honor originally written in blood that had dried and become the color of the *Encyclopaedia Britannica*'s cover. "Wait a minute," they might have said. "This reeks of *Britannica*."

When I get home from the pharmacy, my son is leaned over sideways, drooling more of that gooey pink mix of saliva and blood into the pink dish.

I hold up the white pharmacist sack, rattling pills inside. "How do you feel?"

He shakes his head. Not good. "Did you get me that coconut water?" he asks.

I did.

Frankly, I don't get this coconut water thing. It's a new elixir I know nothing about. (Though I imagine Tarzan must have given Boy coconut water when he had his wisdom teeth out.) I pour a glass of it, roll an opiate from the pill bottle into my hand, and then stop. First food, the nurse said. Then pain medication. I give him a choice of pudding, pudding, or pudding. He decides on the pudding.

It could be teachers were simply in awe of kids who would sit in the library, or at the kitchen table at home, copying long passages from the encyclopedia on whales or the Battle of the Bulge. It was, after all, work. Hard work. Almost as hard as reading and thinking. And maybe they believed there was actual benefit in wholesale theft of the original language. In classical times, students practiced the art of declamation, memorizing and reciting classical speeches. In so doing, they learned about the techniques and skills of famous orators. So when Mrs. Mann or Mrs. Ault or Mrs. Kaufmann looked at writing that was a stylistic reach for me or Randy Glazier or Raymond Robishaw, maybe they thought, *There they go, declaiming again.*

Today no such work is required. Hold down the left mouse button, drag the mouse over the words you want. Copy. Paste. No fear of hand cramp. No threat of carpal tunnel syndrome. *Look, ma, I'm writing.* It's just that easy.

The pain med, it turns out, doesn't do much. My son sinks lower on the couch. Every so often he drools a gooey pink mix of saliva and blood into the pink dish. He loses his sense of humor. He stops talking. I remember that he should take Tylenol—or was it

Motrin?—an hour after the narcotic. While he suffers, I do what any parent today would do. I Google the name of the pain med, linked first to Tylenol, then Motrin.

This is progress. It would never have occurred to my mother to consult *World Book* on a question like this. And I'm pretty sure she felt the same way I did about *Britannica*. But then, in the pre-information age, she would have listened to the nurse and remembered which medication turbocharged the opiate.

On one site I learn that if I give him Tylenol, he will overdose. On another I learn that if I give him Motrin, he might die.

"It hurts," he says.

"Want some more pudding?"

"Mmmf." He turns up the TV and says, barely audible, "Good part." He's watching Nicholas Cage watching an iguana.

The phone rings. It's the oral surgeon's office. How's the patient doing?

Motrin does the job. He sinks still deeper into the couch, expectorates a few gouts of blood into the pink dish, and sips coconut water.

Why wisdom teeth? I wonder, lining up puddings in the fridge.

It's really two questions. Why do we get teeth we don't want or need? And what's wisdom got to do with it? I doubt I would pull down an encyclopedia to answer these questions. But while the patient sleeps, I open my laptop and educate myself.

17

What's Up with
Dramatic-Value Vomit?

My wife and I tuned into *House of Cards* the other night. The scheming Underwoods, Francis and Claire, are being systematically thwarted in the third season. Francis, now President, is asked by his party not to run for a second term. His offer to the solicitor general to accept his nomination to the Supreme Court (and please don't throw your hat in the ring to become a presidential candidate) is rebuffed. Then he is humiliated by visiting Russian President Petrov, who kisses the first lady full on the mouth at a State dinner. And ruthless Claire, the Netflix Lady Macbeth, who would like to be ambassador to the United Nations just in case her husband flops as pres, sasses a senator at her confirmation hearing and loses the vote 52–48.

The Underwoods are not accustomed to losing.

When ever-devious Claire asks her husband for a recess appointment, Francis first says no (he knows her motives), then says yes (his ambition and habit of outfoxing the opposition are too strong), and finally stalks out of the room, leaving Claire happy, surprised, and flummoxed in the White House kitchen.

In the throes of powerful emotion, Claire does what many TV and movie characters do these days. She goes to the sink, lowers her head, and tosses her cookies.

Really, must we vomit? What is this ridiculous trope in modern American film? We're not talking good-natured *Stand by Me* projectile-cherry-pie vomiting for laughs. This is dramatic-value vomit. Joe Queenan, writing for the *Guardian* in 2002, lists the following films with vomit scenes, some with multiple vomits: *Reservoir Dogs, Speed, Hard Target, Vincent and Theo, Blue Velvet, The Godfather, Part III, The Firm, A Perfect World, Memento, The Virgin Suicides, Requiem for a Dream, Almost Famous, The Sixth Sense, 10 Things I Hate About You, Clueless, The Whole Nine Yards,* and *Three to Tango.*

That was 2002. Since then, dramatic-value vomit has snowballed. It's everywhere now, in movies, in TV dramas. Male, female, it's an equal opportunity gesture. The idea is you get to know the character's interior by finding out what she had for lunch. Your husband is leaving you? Pull up the wastebasket and un-eat. Lost the family savings in an investment scam? That calls for a histrionic horf. Can't pay the mob the money you owe? Time to talk to Ralph on the big white telephone.

Granted, there is medical literature on stress vomiting. Dr. Tracy A. Dennis in the department of psychology at Hunter College cites powerful emotions, such as anger, shame, fear, and delight, as possible triggers of stress vomit.

"When we're angry," he notes, "our heart rate increases, adrenaline flows, blood pressure spikes, and we 'see red.'"

And then comes gastrointestinal distress, and possibly, emesis (vomiting). Vomit literature also treats cyclic vomiting syndrome, a malady affecting 2 percent of school-age children and an increasing number of adults, and emetophobia, or fear of vomiting, which afflicts up to 1.7–3.1 percent of males and 6–7 percent of females. Vomit lit also refers, at least in passing, to an atmospheric death metal band named Emesis, with such hit songs as "Moulded Blood," "Sacrifice, the Flesh," "Bring Your Slasherhook," and "Raped in the Crypt." Guaranteed to produce a headache and, in some listeners, induce vomiting.

So stress vomit, not to be confused with flu- or migraine- or pregnancy- or motion sickness– or alcohol- or death metal–induced vomit, is a thing. But how did de-fooding for dramatic effect become so pervasive?

You have to wonder if there's a checklist of devices that writers, directors, and producers consult, to which dramatic-value vomit has been added.

Car chase?

Yup.

Exploding car crash?

Got it.

Character talking to himself in the mirror?

Check.

Run out of bullets and throw your gun at your target?

Missed that one.

Obligatory shower scene?

Is there a movie made these days that doesn't show a character standing in the shower, water splashing on his or her head? Steam rises around them, signaling deep conflict, confusion; water gutters in the drain, signaling water—and hope or love or faith or resolve—going down the drain. It's like a time-out. Hang on, viewer. We'll get back to the movie in just a minute.

My first recollection of a shower scene, after Alfred Hitchcock's in *Psycho*, is from *The Big Chill*. In the opening scenes of that movie we see Glenn Close sitting on the floor of the shower. Steam rises around her, signaling confusion. But wait, that's not all: the Glenn Close character is weeping. The shower scene means something; it's there for a purpose. And Hitchcock puts poor Janet Leigh's character in the shower not for a pause but to set the scene for the next dramatic action.

A few months ago I watched part of *Enemy*, a murky film with Jake Gyllenhaal as a Toronto professor confronting his doppelgänger. His look-alike does a number on him. Should he follow himself?

Should he reach out and make contact? What does all this mean? Gyllenhaal's character is so conflicted he has to shower twice in the first forty-five minutes of the film. Something told me, as I was changing the channel, that dramatic-value vomit was in his future. But this dramatic-value vomit is a modern thing, a movie/TV thing. Entertainments past? I'm pretty sure no one vomits in Shakespeare for dramatic effect. In all thirty-seven plays put together, in a total of 807 scenes, the word "vomit" occurs only six times, "puke" only twice. And usually it's figurative vomit.

You might expect to find some emesis in Shakespeare, as it figured prominently in the practice of medicine in his time. To keep the four humors in balance and to restore the patient to health, doctors prescribed emetics to induce vomiting, or laxatives, or proceeded to a salubrious bloodletting. In "Sonnet 118," Shakespeare writes, "We sicken to shun sickness when we purge."

The closest we come to dramatic-value vomit in Shakespeare is when Hamlet, standing in a graveyard in act 5, scene 1, holds up Yorick's skull and addresses him/it: "a fellow of infinite jest, of most excellent fancy. He hath borne me on his back a thousand times, and now, how abhorred in my imagination it is! *My gorge rises at it*" (my emphasis). If Hamlet were to hurl, it would be justified. But in the all the Hamlets I've ever seen, he doesn't. It would be superfluous. Hamlet can say what's on his mind. There's no need to show us. Possibly in contemporary productions, a director of *Hamlet* would suggest, "My gorge rises is your motivation to rush downstage and honk into the pit."

Please don't make it so.

No, in Shakespeare, there are no vomits, dramatic-value or otherwise.

And fortunately, Shakespeare also predates the shower as dramatic time-out. If there were ever a shower scene candidate, it's Macbeth. When he asks, contemplating his murder of Duncan, "Will all great Neptune's ocean wash the blood clean from my hand?" you might picture him thinking that while slumped against the tile walls in the castle shower, steam rising around him, signaling confusion, incarnadine waters guttering in the drain.

So too Lady Macbeth, with steam rising around her in the shower, might deliver the lines: "What, will these hands ne'er be clean?" and "All the perfumes of Arabia will not sweeten this little hand." She scrubs her hands, asks: "Who would have thought the old man to have had so much blood in him."

Who wants to pause for a shower?

You might think the dread Lady, as she becomes more unhinged, would vomit at least once, before her exit.

She doesn't need a shower or dramatic-value vomit. She just uses her words, and the show goes on.

18

Old Houses, New Residents

A couple of gay guys have moved into the Berlin house. As far as I know, this is something new in the neighborhood.

The houses in our neighborhood go by the names of the families who lived in them. There's the Whittaker house, the Hawkins house, the Stahl house. We've lived in the Hawthorne house for twenty-six years. Before us were the Youngs, who didn't stay long enough to give their name to the house. You have to live in the house for years and fill it with kids and then empty it of kids. Once it's empty and you're left wandering around listening to echoes, it gets your name. I guess we're there.

But I've thought lately, especially since I've been watching a lot of *Doc Martin*, that it might be nice to just drop the "The," elevate the "H," and call our place "Hawthorne House." Have a little sign painted and nailed above the front door. The shortened name would give our house a kind of stature, make it seem English-y. "We're having a little gathering at Hawthorne House on Saturday. Care to join us?"

For about ten minutes I entertained the idea of giving the house its own name. I found an English-house-name generator online. I was asked to choose three terms I could associate with the house. I chose "good view," "trees," and "sheep." Okay, there are no sheep around, but the atmosphere is bucolic, so think metaphorical sheep. See those squirrels? Next, what is the house near? Down the hill behind us is a minor pond that gets warm and gicky in August, home to a couple of large, primordial turtles. "Pond" was not a choice. I went with lake. Finally, a color that relates to the house. When our son was three, he always referred to it as "our blue house," possibly because at that time the leaky cedar shakes, once slate-gray, had been so weathered and generally sun-blasted they appeared kind of blue.

I clicked "Okay" and then came the names, none of which seemed apt. "House at the End of the Vale." Too isolated. "Court of the Rushes." Too bustling. "Lake of the Swan." Too Yeats. "Blue River." Huh? Was I supposed to put "cottage" or "house" on the end of these? Blue River Cottage? Lake of the Swan House? House at the End of the Vale . . . House ? There were lots more choices, all of them terrible. I had a feeling we were heading for "Love Shack in the Glen . . . House."

No sooner did the gay guys move into the Berlin house I began to notice traffic over there, first cars, then trucks. On the side of the trucks I saw the future: marble countertops, hardwood floors, elite plumbing. Yard lights squirted out of flower beds newly plump with impatiens. Urns and potted plants appeared.

I rode by on my bike one day. One of the new owners was outside applying sealer to the paving stones with a roller.

"Rick."

"John."

"You live in the Berlin house," I said.

"The Berlins," he said.

"Three owners back."

"Well, there's a lot of work to do."

"It's looking good," I said. Before the Berlins was the guy from FEMA. Before him the FBI agent. Ten years back, in its prime, it was the Berlin house because the Berlins had lived there forever.

He said he liked the Berlin house better than the FBI house. While we were talking, a van pulled in the driveway. Custom Kitchen and Bath.

So there goes the neighborhood, I thought, but in a good way. Except pretty soon, our house would start to look so dowdy and ordinary and, well, hetero.

There are also new occupants in the house directly across the street from us, in the Baker's house. It's called that not because of a family named Baker. The historical owner was a baker, an Armenian kind-of-misanthrope who left for work in the predawn hours for twenty-five years, walked his black dog in the yard, and did not respond much to friendly overtures. I only know his name was Mike. I never wanted to say "Mike's house." It seemed familiar.

These new residents of the Baker's house are shadowy figures. They are young. They have lots of cars. They never seem to be home. I think they are renters. Occasionally I see a young man smoking on the sidewalk outside the garage. When I walked out to get the newspaper one morning I heard him talking on his cell phone. Actually, he was yelling. "How the fuck can someone make that much money in sales?" It was 5:00 a.m.

I was getting ready to water the rhododendrons and geraniums the other day when, looking out the living room window, I saw a lawn chair in the Baker's yard and a young woman lying on it, in a swimsuit. I don't know what I saw, I really don't, but what I thought I saw was a young woman sunbathing topless in the Baker's yard. That would also be something completely new in the neighborhood. What about the small children living next door, in the Adida house? What if they saw a sunbathing topless woman? We have binoculars, strictly ornamental things, sitting on a windowsill in the living room. For a second, I considered fetching them, just to verify. Was that a strap I saw on her right shoulder? I pictured the young woman sitting up, applying lotion to her bosom, and then looking across her lawn, across the road and our lawn, meeting my binocular eyes and waving, holding up her hand, making a loose fist, and extending her middle finger in my specific direction. I didn't look. Really, I didn't.

The baker was still living in that house when my wife and I backed down our driveway early one morning some twenty years ago. We drove south to the airport, boarded a plane, and flew to New Jersey. Alan, a friend of ours, was dead. Maybe our most important friend, the one responsible for bringing us together in college. We landed in Newark and drove to the Jersey shore, to the home he had shared with Allen, his partner.

It was our first time meeting this new Allen, who told us that he had bought a funeral plot close to a big tree in the cemetery, which he thought Alan would like. He told us that before his final hospitalization, our Alan had flown to Arizona to see his parents, to try again to explain his life to them, to try to reconcile and to prepare both them and himself for his death, and that he had been once again terribly, even brutally rejected.

On this a warm summer day we sat on the porch drinking lemonade. We met surviving Allen's parents, who were warm and gentle and, like their son, haunted by the terrible last weeks and days. When the time came, we drove to a funeral chapel. The casket was closed. There was no ceremony. We just had time together, with our Alan's small acquired family.

Before we left, Allen pointed at a table and told us we could take some photos of our Alan. There were a lot of them. Help ourselves.

We approached the table. There were, indeed, a lot of photos. In all of them, our Alan was dressed as a woman. He wore a blond wig, a sleeveless dress. He mugged lasciviously at the camera. We picked up one image after another, looked at each other, and set them down. That wasn't how we wanted to see him. It wasn't how we remembered him.

I wish now that we'd taken one of those photographs. I would have put it away, probably with the letter he wrote telling us he was sick, a letter I've never been able to read a second time. Probably I wouldn't ever look at that photo again, either, of his other self, the one he evidently wanted to leave us with, but it would be there.

Old houses, new residents.

One Thursday morning I'm taking trash down to the road. It's 6:00 a.m. The residents of the Baker's house set their trash out the night before, in flimsy plastic bags the crows plunder. It's not uncommon to see bones and eggshells in the street in front of their house. I glance over at the Berlin house and check out their garbage can, which is brand new, more like a vase (rhyme it with Oz) than a can.

Who are these people? Do we want to know? Can we ever know? We could try.

"Hey, we're having a little gathering at Hawthorne House on Saturday. Care to join us?"

And they might say, "Sorry, we're busy." Or they might say, "Who are the Hawthornes?"

Our response would have to be, "Really, we have no idea. For the time being, it's our house. Come to our house."

19

Bee Spree

Yesterday I committed apicide. And I took pleasure in it.

Actually, this wasn't my first time. When it comes to bees, I am a serial killer, an apicidal maniac.

Every so often, bees appear and take up residence in and around our house. I'm cutting the lawn and see one disappear under the bay window on the back of the house. On the next pass with the mower, I see two or three, or five or ten more come and go. This summer they have infiltrated the house through a gap in some shingles, just above the front porch. I watch the traffic for weeks. I'm not sure where they're going, but I know I don't want them in there. Mostly these are little guys—I would say honeybees. They are not aggressive. I can get in their little faces. They are not distracted. They are all about their business.

A few years ago carpenter bees made a home in the cedar fascia and soffit outside our screened-in porch in the back. Carpenter bees are big brutes, the size of bumblebees, with broad shoulders and a fierce buzz. They cast a big shadow, a menacing, inky blot that moves across the screen in midafternoon. They drill a perfectly round five-eighths-inch hole in the wood and make a ninety degree turn. Then they bore into the wood. During the worst of this invasion, some afternoons when I sat inside and it was perfectly quiet, I am sure I heard them—*tick tick tick*—gnashing their bee teeth, gnawing on our cedar.

The popular solution, recommended by the Michigan State University gardening center, is to use a turkey baster to puff Sevin, a fine, lethal powder, into the holes they bore. I can't imagine why this method is popular. Gravity works against you. In the injection phase of the campaign, you squeeze and hold the baster bulb, lower the baster tip into the poison canister, and let the bulb go, drawing the powder up into the baster tube. Then you hold the baster aloft, insert the tip of the baster into the hole the carpenter bees have bored, and vigorously squeeze the bulb to puff poison up into the carpenter hole. The problem is that the powder obeys gravity and your Sevin spills back down the tube of the baster. It's hard to get the goods to the bees. To foil these pests, I roll small cotton swabs in the powder and insert them in the holes. Coming home from work, a bee has to drag his weary wings through the poison and past the swab and, in the process, hauls the swab into the hive, if it is, in fact, a hive. Thus do I deal out doom. It works.

Honeybees are more challenging. There's more of them. For some time now I've used a heavy vacuum cleaner, a shop vac, running a few inches of water into the bottom of the can, positioning the end of the hose at the front door of their hive, and letting the appliance run. Poor bees. As they approach their home and power down, slowing their flight to enter the hive, they are sucked into the vacuum cleaner. The bees leaving the hive on a search mission, they too are powerless to avoid the suction and the hose. In a few hours' time, you can dispatch a great many bees—hundreds, I would say. Once I've depleted the population, I give the nest a generous shot of Raid and mew up the queen and survivors, hoping to finish them off. I don't like to think of their demise, the maelstrom of air and water, the confusion and terror of their last moments. But then, neither do I like to think of their settlements inside the walls of my house. It's my house. I will fight to maintain the boundary between my world and theirs.

When I was in college, a professor who had recently become a father talked candidly about his protection fantasies. He said he lay awake at night imagining what he would do if an intruder broke into his home and threatened his wife and baby. He described these musings, with a hint of embarrassment, as his "*Straw Dogs* fantasies" (for the Sam Peckinpah movie in theaters at the time, an orgy of violence starring brainy little Dustin Hoffman). "You will understand one day," he said to us. When I became a father, I did understand. And in this way, I also vaguely understand those who arm themselves and celebrate the Second Amendment. They live rich fantasy lives. They are their own well-regulated militia.

But bees.

Not just bees, but honeybees, symbols of impending environmental collapse. I know we need them. I know I should call someone. There must be a bee whisperer out there, some ingenious and generous soul who can conjure them, lure them to safety so they can fulfill themselves. Or in an ideal world we would learn to coexist. In exchange for my no-shop-vac, no-Raid pledge, the bees would vouchsafe a no-sting, enjoy-our-honey pledge. But that's nonsense.

When I hear the buzz, I go on high alert. They can live where they want, and they definitely have a place in the scheme of things. But around and in my house? No. I will stand my ground.

20

Hello, Mr. President

In this dream, I'm having a plane crash.

I'm sitting in the full lotus position, dropping through space, alone. It's cold and dark, windy and noisy. I'm confused at first, but then I get it. Someone else is going to have the crash. I just happen to be outside the plane, falling. I gather that my death is imminent, and somehow I know that I'm falling toward the sea. At first I feel terrible regret about all I'm going to miss in this life—my wife, my kids, my grandchildren. Then, after a few thousand feet of freefall, comes resignation, acceptance. I picture the eventual search detail looking for me. And suddenly, in this dream, I'm glad I wore my new long-sleeve jersey from the Gap. It's bright. It makes me easier to see, in parking lots, for example.

I picture my wife in a search plane, its engines droning, a headset clamped to her ears, binoculars pressed to her face, as she surveys thousands of square miles of desolate ocean.

A uniformed guy sitting next to her says, "What was he wearing?"

"His new shirt from Gap," she says.

"What color?"

"Kind of a . . . cerulean," she says.

Uniformed guy nods, thinks, gives up. "Just gimme a color," he says. My wife the color theorist explains that it's a kind of blue, a hue, really, somewhere between pure blue and cyan. She says that I looked good in it (choking up when she says this), that I was easily recognizable, in parking lots, for example.

Crap, I think. *Blue! They'll never find me now, lost in the blue, blue sea.* And then the dream fades to black. I don't hit the sea. I don't die.

Experts say you don't die if your dream fall is completed. I'll have to take them at their word. I've never actually finished the fall. I've never hit the sidewalk after falling from a tall building. I've never crashed into the desert in a poof of dust, Wile E. Coyote–like, after falling from a cliff. Even when, barely asleep, I stub my toe or fall off a bicycle or slip on a patch of ice, triggering that annoying hypnagogic jerk that wakes us up, I never totally fall. I don't skin a knee or bump my face. Is there pain in dreams? I don't recall feeling pain in a dream. Is there death? All those reports of seemingly healthy people who die in their sleep—you start to wonder. Who's to say they didn't dream-fall to their dream- and actual death? There's no test for that.

Experts also say a person is likely to have a falling dream a half a dozen times or so in a lifetime. Here's a list, courtesy of those who study dreams, of the most common recurring dream themes: falling, flying, losing your teeth; being chased or naked or late; water dreams; test dreams.

Everyone must have their own list of recurring dreams. I have a recurring house-filling-up-with-water dream. Usually it's a house on a hillside. It's someone else's house; nevertheless I feel a strong sense of responsibility and desperation in the dream as I slosh from room to room, eventually escaping out the back door onto a veranda, where water reaches my waist.

There's the recurring airport/travel dream. I've missed my flight, the airport morphs into a foreign city I vaguely recognize. I feel like I should know my way around as I wander from room to room, from street to street, invariably at night. It all looks familiar, in an Escher-like way, as if I'm in a dreamscape I've crossed in the past, yet I am hopelessly lost. Then there's the sitting-on-the-toilet-in-the-driveway dream, and, inexplicably (but what's truly explicable in a dream?) the recurring Jimmy Carter dream.

The first time I dreamed about Jimmy Carter, he had been out of office for years. In the dream I was in my hometown, at a party at the Coy house, on the corner of Fifth and Church Streets. It was a summer night. There was a volleyball net in the backyard, though I do not remember the Coy family as volleyball enthusiasts. No one was playing volleyball in the dream. I was standing outside, swatting mosquitos, probably looking for the beer keg, when Jimmy Carter walked around the corner of the house and across the backyard. He walked right past me.

"Hello, Mr. President," I said.

He looked up and nodded at me. He didn't answer.

In later dreams of Carter, when I have greeted him, always with the same, "Hello, Mr. President," he still doesn't answer, even though I feel like we're kind of getting to know each other.

Now that I think of it, it seems like no one talks to me in my dreams. I talk to them. I greet them, I ask them questions, sometimes I beseech them. No one answers. I guess they don't know what to say.

The problem with dreams, Richard Francis Kuhns has pointed out, is it's hard to get out of them. "Dream constitutes an inescapable story," Kuhns says, "which must be attended to. As the dream is dreamt the dreamer cannot be distracted from the dream as one might be in listening to a story that is read or spoken out loud." You can't change the channel; you can't even lower the volume. You can't ignore a dream that's happening to you. You're trapped in it.

A few weeks ago, my wife had a minor episode of night terror,[1] crying out in her sleep. When he was little, my son went through a phase of night terrors. We would hear moans and muffled screams in the dead of night. When it happens, you have the uncanny feeling the person you know and love is far from you, unreachable, almost someone else, as if possessed. Even waking them, you can't quite get to them. And for a while they can't get back to you.

A loved one's night terror is your family's own sci-fi or horror show, a disquieting, homey mystery.

On the other hand, I tend more toward night humors, find myself waking up thinking, *What was that?* And: *How do I go back?*

Sometimes we know we are dreaming. We're in it, the way Kuhns has it, but we know we're in it. We have distance, perspective. But no control. In dream literature this state is referred to as "lucid dreaming." The term was coined by a Dutch psychiatrist named Frederik van Eeden. The definitive text on lucid dreaming seems to be Marquis d'Hervey de Saint-Denys's *Les rêves et les moyens de les diriger: Observations pratiques* (Dreams and the Ways to Direct Them: Practical Observations, 1867). It sounds like an instruction manual. Those who develop skill at lucid dreaming are called oneironauts.

I probably won't read Denys's guide.

The Lucidity Institute offers a course in lucid dreaming. On the Institute website we are told, "The two essentials to learning lucid dreaming are motivation and effort." That sounds like work.

I don't want to become a oneironaut. For one thing, it's an ugly word. For another, what if becoming a oneironaut diminished the dream, undermining the element of surprise? Even my recurring dreams are not re-runs. I want to keep them that way.

---

1 I prefer the term night terror to "nightmare" because the latter seems needlessly sexist. (Nightmare, according to *Oxford Living Dictionaries*: "Middle English denoting a female evil spirit thought to lie upon and suffocate sleepers: from night + Old English *mære* 'incubus.'")

21

Chemical Neutral

"What you do," the tree man says, "is get some Great Stuff. Fill the tree up with it to keep the water out of it."

We're standing beside an apple tree. Well, half an apple tree. We have three of them left, all senior citizens feeling their years. Our house sits on property that was part of a large orchard in the nineteenth century. Gradually most of our neighbors have cut down their apple trees. The one now reduced to half its former self has looked haggard and dry for a few years—part of it, anyway. This spring I was going to lop off a dead chunk of it. Then a wind storm came through the area. There were enough leaves in the tree for it to resist, but it lost its worse half. When I got up Father's Day morning, there it was, broken, half the tree bowing to the grass. A deep hollow in the trunk yawned out of the gap, a void four inches in diameter and twenty-some inches deep. Before cooking lunch that Sunday, I cut the dead wood into pieces with my chain saw and hauled them to the road.

I've got a guy over to look at the tree.

He says, "Keep the water out, it'll last a while." He looks up at the tree, nods, and says, "Great Stuff."

I do not love an apple tree. We had one in our yard when I was growing up. One was enough. Every fall my brother and I picked up rotten apples and trundled them to the garden in a wheelbarrow. Our parents grew a big vegetable garden. They also had rows of backbreaking strawberries and a long stand of thorny, obstreperous raspberry bushes that grew rampant and were frightfully prolific. Relatives would come or townspeople would stop by for a visit. Our mother would hand us a bowl and say, "Go pick Vernon and Matty a couple quarts." When the misery of nature's bounty had passed into fall, there remained the apple tree. It was tall, craggy, and usually loaded. The grass under the tree was thin and sickly. All my hatred of the garden could be invested in that beast. Eventually the tree came down and a basketball rim went up.

Great Stuff is a Dow Chemical product. It comes in a yellow can. It's under pressure. You screw a six-inch tube onto a tip in the top of the can, bend the tip, and a stream of goop the color of a pastry chef's egg cream comes squirting out. The active ingredient in Great Stuff is Great Stuff, plus air. And it is lively. I emptied a can into the tree, watched it expand and fill the void, and saw I would need reinforcements. I went back to Ace Hardware for two more cans, emptying both of them into the cavern. Then I went in the house. When I looked out the kitchen window, I saw the tree vomiting Great Stuff in slow-mo. Great Stuff stuck to the side of the tree. Great Stuff puddled on the ground.

There should be a sign on the can. In large letters: DON'T TOUCH GREAT STUFF.

I grabbed what I could find—a paper bag, some newspapers, a piece of cardboard—thinking I would just trowel a nice finish on Great Stuff.

It was not a friend to the trowel.

By accident, I touched it. I think it touched me on purpose.

It was sticky.

Forget soap and water. Only gasoline would take it off, which I poured over my hands at the edge of the driveway, cursing the Great Stuff stuck to my fingers, to my flip-flops and shorts.

That day a headline caught my attention, about the oceans being near death. The oceans, too vast for the mind to contain, a symbol of infinity. How do we succeed in exhausting and murdering infinity? Fished out, polluted, their ecosystems destabilized by temperature change and increased carbon dioxide levels, the oceans, it is said, could be dead within a generation.

Lake Erie came to mind. The dead lake. And, spoiled by Dow Chemical, the Tittabawassee River—its stench, its spectral clouds of steam rising in subzero temperatures, its hideous population of grimy carp we fished and dragged up on the banks as kids, monstrous fish we recoiled from and kicked with disgust back in the water.

I've sailed on Lake Erie and eaten its perch. It's made a comeback. The Tittabawassee too has experienced a rebirth. Walleye run up the river to spawn. I can't quite take it in, the walleye, the river's rebirth without birth defects. My brother said not long ago he put a boat in the river north of town and by accident (any physical contact with the river was, would be, and must always be an accident), stepped in the water. His foot broke the surface tension of the muck in the bottom, he said, and what came up was a dark, smoky cloud of disturbed sediment and the smell. The smell of dead river, the smell of Dow.

We were ten years in this house when we lost the first apple tree. It was the biggest of the four, and it was beautiful, the color and texture of its bark alternating between slate and coal, its herculean branches rising gracefully and powerfully above the yard. Mowing the lawn one day, I noticed business around the base of the tree—ant business. When a big branch later dropped off, I saw in the hollow of the tree more than just business. I saw ant industry, hunting and gathering, a diverse thriving economy predicated on the destruction of the tree.

We'd had ants in the house—big fellows—long-bodied, lusty black carpenter ants that crunch when you step on them. Every spring and summer, we'd find them with a jolt of surprise, on the floor behind a door, on the kitchen counter. Sitting on the couch, you'd feel a tickle across your arm as one jogged over it, heading for a sofa cushion.

When I told my wife the big apple was full of ants, she was resolute.

Within a week, we had a crew in the yard. The guys came out at the end of the day. They must have figured: one tree.

The top branches came down and then the lower branches, all of them full of ants.

When the workers cut the base of the tree four feet above ground, a crater was opened, and from it black ants poured—a geyser of ants, clouds of them fuming down the sides of the tree. Even the tree guys were shaken.

As an adult, I grew to tolerate the apple trees. Come fall, I had to clean up after them, filling plastic grocery bags with apples, bags I then lugged to the road to be carried away on Thursdays. Apple waste. Every year my mother-in-law would look up into the trees and ask why we didn't eat them.

"Because they're wormy," I said.

She would point way up in the tree. "That one," she'd say, "looks good."

Yes, it was red. But no, I'd say, they're all full of worms. We would have to spray. Our neighbor sprayed his peach trees, valiantly trying to keep away the bugs, trusting the poison to do its work, but eventually he gave up on growing perfect, bug-free, poisoned fruit. But they had become beautiful, these old, infested trees. Some summer evenings late into dusk I'd walk the yard, enjoy the deep liquid green, stand among our trees—silent, dark hulks that seemed more than present. They seemed to give off something. I liked to think of them as possessed by spirits. Or as receptacles in which wandering spirits could reside. Maybe the spirits of our loved ones, near us. Maybe just the spirits of other trees. There was a vibration. You were with them, the trees and their occupants. You did not feel alone.

The day after I inject my apple tree with foam, I awaken to a tree with a goiter. Great Stuff has continued to boil over, though the rate has slowed and the pressure has subsided, causing the tree to form a protuberance the size of a volleyball on the side of the tree. The growth looks like a giant meringue. Or a tumor. At first I'm horrified and sickened, but then I'm excited by the possibilities this thing offers. I could paint a face on it and call it the spirit of the tree. Or I could just leave it as it is, see what happens to it over time. Judging from the efficacy of Dow engineering, I might have to wait a few thousand years to detect any change, as I'm sure it is heat-, cold-, rain-, snow-, bird-, and squirrel-resistant. The only thing to do is cut it off.

The ideal tool for this blobectomy is a drywall saw, which makes a clean excision. There is some blobdust.

I'm left with part tree, part cannoli. To discolor the foam, I spray it with gray Krylon primer. "No drips, no runs, no errors," it says on the can. As I spray, Great Stuff begins to tick, and I'm afraid that Dow and Krylon do not make nice, but in the end, nothing happens. That's my goal, to hold the tree in chemical neutral, give it a chance to live and die a modern death.

22

Pure Corn

My daughter has come home to put the finishing touches on wedding plans. This means periods of frenzy, elation, and angst. Lists, invitations, dresses, music, food, flowers. Suddenly the time to decide is now, or yesterday. But today she is calm, which means I am calm. She's been tasting cakes and has found one she likes, made with corn.

"It was delicious," she says. "And so unusual."

I'm standing at the kitchen sink, peeling a carrot. A few weeks ago I let a TV foodist lecture me about the benefits of natural carrots. I'm peeling a virtuous carrot.

"No one eats wedding cake," I say.

"Because it's always so bad," she says. "I want mine to be good."

She's just finished culinary school. To watch her prepare a meal, even in our kitchen, is a little like going to the ballet. All that art. Her grub is so good, I want to stuff my bouche.

What she's thinking, what I'm thinking, is that corn cake is edgy. But neither of us will say it. Some words, when they've been repeated billions of times in speech and in print, and repeated with that knowing wink (it's edgy to say "edgy") totally lose their little jolt of electricity. At the end of the day, even if we're both on the same page, neither of us will ever say "edgy."

This baker, from Ann Arbor, makes cakes that will please the locavore. All natural ingredients, preferably local; whole wheat flour. These are correct cakes.

"What was your cake?" she asks.

Rum torte. I would have been happy with one those white monstrosities that look like a drum set, preferably with an edible bride and groom on top. My wife worked with the baker, an amiable German immigrant named Peter, telling him exactly what she wanted, something simple, none of that sugary frosting, a cake people would want to eat. So we ended up with these little brown rounds of cake, all arranged in a circle, like a diorama of huts in a sustainable village. At some point in the evening, we posed and nudged slices of it into each other's mouths. It was good. A year after we were married, my wife produced a shrunken hovel of wedding cake from the freezer, which we thawed and ate. I detected no rum. It tasted freezery.

It's not news. We're on the threshold—all of us, you too—of a long, silent scream. What's happened to food production in this country? Whatta we got to eat?

My first awareness of this skittishness about food came years ago. My grandmother brought home a frying pan coated with Teflon. My grandfather, a cast-iron-frying-pan man, was skeptical. In the first plate of eggs he ate, he said he could taste the Teflon. "Daddy gets notions," my grandmother said.

Bad eggs, he said. Bring back the old pan.

He shaved with a straight razor and patted his cheeks with alcohol when he finished, emerging from the bathroom with a shiny chin, smelling clean and flammable. He farmed and drove a rural mail delivery route. He milked six cows year-round, calling them home every evening, tending to them in a manner both businesslike and loving. They stood in their stalls; he sat on a stool next to them and milked. I remember wondering how something as good as milk could come from a space both sweetly redolent of hay and reeking of piss and cow pie. But it did.

I became suspicious of our milk a while back. Modern milk, store milk. Industrial milk. This milk didn't taste good in a glass, in cereal, in coffee, anywhere. I paid $1.99 a gallon at Kroger for a plasticky, hormonious imposter. The color was right. Nothing else.

Home from college one Friday night, my daughter asked why I didn't buy the good stuff.

"What good stuff?" I said.

In time I was converted, not without a fight, to organic milk. I hated the idea. I hated those happy cows on the carton, cows that mooed "just say no to druggy, industrial milk." I hated the phony celebration of Farmer Families, which I saw as a crock of advertising bull on par with Amish chickens (some of those birds, I happen to know, are Presbyterian). Mostly I hated paying even more for milk, for something that was supposed to be good and cheap and inviolable.

The first milk I bought, in elementary school, cost two cents a carton and made sandwiches, cupcakes, and cookies taste better. Do kids even drink milk now? Does milk go with Gogurt and Doritos?

Corn cake. Why not?

Corn is local. Corn is sweet. Corn is a tidy food: eight hundred kernels in sixteen rows.

Corn has wide appeal. It's every kid's favorite vegetable. (Except corn is not a vegetable. My sources tell me, "Every kernel of corn is a fruit." Whatever. All the better for cake.)

Read up on corn, and you'll be charmed. Maybe because the corn plant itself is so tall and stately. Unlike meager beans crouching in their fields, corn has stature. Corn becomes a forest you can get lost in. Read between the lines, and you'll see there's romance in corn. Not us romancing in the corn. The corn romancing in itself. It grows its own silk and has tassels that release pollen. On warm

July evenings, given a light breeze, a great green orgy takes place in those corn fields, a love-in that Purdue agronomist R. L. Nielson says can last for up to fourteen days. All those midwesterners sitting on porches long summer nights: they're not watching the corn grow. It's way better than that.

But corn cake? I'm locavore enough to know that for a January wedding, someone's importing her corn. And what corn is it? Corn in the can? Corn in the freezer? Long-lasting corn that, like an industrial tomato, can wait forever if need be and still be fresh? No food produced today is more messed with than corn. It's Frankenstein in the fields, an environmental disaster waiting to happen. Or maybe already happening. Or maybe it's just corn.

The next night my daughter comes home with another box of cake samples. These are from a different baker. We eat dinner, push back from the table, and turn our attention to sweets.

"I'm just afraid people will be weirded out by corn cake," she says. She hands me a little confection the size of a hockey puck. There are six or seven samples to try, all with a brownish frosting that reminds me of our wedding cake.

"Butter cream?" I ask. Then I take bite.

She nods. "Heavenly."

"That can be risky," my wife says. One bite obliterates her.

The cake sample is good. They're all good. They're all fruity, cakey things. We take turns taking bites and learn that the active ingredient, the animating principle, is Nutella. Somewhere, sometime, a genius had the idea of bringing together chocolate and hazelnut. The combination was more than inspired food engineering. It was art. It was a good marriage.

I ask for another bite and realize I should probably have a glass of postmodern milk.

23

Fly

It's four days since the rented Penske truck pulled out of the driveway. The second and final load. We now have space in the attic. We have one fewer mattress in the basement. Some great books will be permanently checked out of our library. Most of those budget Italian ceramics my wife has been buying at Home Goods, for pasta or fruit or flowers, for anything wanting some easy elegance, are packed up and gone. In the first few weeks after my kids learned to drive, as they pulled away, I stood in the driveway with my heart pounding in my chest, praying they would come home in one piece. Then I got used to it.

"See ya later," they'd say.

And I'd say, "Yeah."

This is like that. The first time the Penske truck leaves, I feel the pounding sensation. The second time I'm sort of used to it. But this time is also different. To get to where my daughter and her husband are going takes nine hours. "See ya soon," she says.

Four days later, early one Thursday morning, I'm lugging trash out to the road. This one bag I pick up and drop, there's something in it that goes *pop!* When I hoist the bag, liquid dribbles from a bottom corner. It's been hot, in the nineties for a few weeks. Garbage will deliquesce. I walk down to the road with the bag, dreading the cleanup ahead of me.

By the time I'm back, the smell of peppermint pervades the garage. What broke, I'm guessing, is a bottle of mouthwash. Who throws away mouthwash? I daub at the spilled liquid with a wet paper towel, which amounts to massaging the liquid into the floor. I toss a bucket of water across the cement and rough up the sticky spots with a broom. The garage now smells like a candy shop. So does the mudroom just inside in the house.

It's almost August. This outbreak of sweetness worries me.

Some time ago, two years in a row we got an influx of flies in the garage, both times in early August. We've had influxes—chipmunks in the attic, finches on a window ledge, starlings in the apple tree. One time I came home to find a grackle in the house. These invasions come and go. But flies—creatures of manure and death, pests that make a person shrivel—flies come to stay. They move in and are shitty company. You can't murder them fast enough.

The idea that we can create an impermeable barrier between human space and the natural world, when you examine it, seems like the highest order of folly. We do a pretty good job of keeping the rain out, the cold and hot out, but every so often there are reminders of our limits. I move a dish in the sink, and an earwig goes looking for cover. I open a cupboard door and see an ant going about his business. The other day I was working on the back porch, screened in to keep the bugs out. I looked up from my work to see a hornet buzzing around, like a drone waiting for attack coordinates to be radioed from central command.

Around ten years ago we noticed a couple of fleas in an upstairs bathroom, and then we noticed more; in a couple of days there were clouds of them. An exterminator came. He guessed there was a dead animal in the wall, probably one of those chipmunks. We were invited to leave the house for five or six hours. When we came home, along the floor and the edges of the window frame was a white powdery substance, which we were instructed to leave for a few days. The stuff worked. No more fleas. No flea carcasses. No dead-flea-eating fleas. Our sacrosanct space, now slightly poisonous, was restored.

The housefly (*Musca domestica*) is a sleazy little beast. It's hairy. It has awful "compound eyes" that, through no fault of its own, are huge, red, and, for want of a better term, buggy. That thing protruding downward from its head—a complex apparatus consisting of maxillary palps, labium, labellum, pseudotracheae, and (ugh) tip—is used to import shit, rot, putrescence, and other delectables into its body. Thirty-six hours after emerging from its pupa (a word I do not like and hope never to write again), it is ready for sex. A fly will live two weeks to a month in the wild. Do the math. They are prodigiously randy, just babies when they start having sex, each female loaded with five hundred eggs. Humans evolved some two hundred thousand years ago and have been full-blown *Homo sapiens* for around fifty thousand years. Flies have been around for some sixty-five million years. Where they buzz, they buzz with a kind of confidence we can only imagine.

Pulling into my garage one day in August some years ago, I noticed a buzz. On closer inspection, I saw them, a few dozen flies looking out the garage windows. They seemed unworthy of much concern. A few days later, the buzz was louder, more varied, a pestilent philharmonic. There were enough flies on the window I could swat at them with the *New York Times* and dispatch half a dozen at a time. The others, listless, probably postcoitally lethargic, didn't fly away. In five minutes, the floor was dotted with dead flies, which I swept up and tossed out in the yard.

The next day they were back. I used the sports section for fly slaughter.

The day after that the flies were all over the windows and dotted the door from the garage into the house.

"Bleach," my wife said. That's her solution to everything.

The next morning I sprayed the windows with bleach and wiped them down, hopeful if not satisfied that I'd outsmarted the flies. I put the garbage cans outside.

Next day, on windows, on the door: flies. And, to my horror, on the window just inside the house: flies.

I looked for home remedies online. They were quaint.

Basil plants by the door will rid u of the flies.

Good to know, thanks.

*I always use apple cidar vinager [*sic*]. Put some in a bowl with a drop of dawn dishsoap and place it where the flies are. They love it and it also helps with bad odors.*

Great, I'll get right on that. (Great for fruit flies, not for the big brutes.)

Fill sandwich baggie half full of water, hang over any door which leads from outside to inside (hang bag over outside of door). The fly sees its reflection in the water, is scared off. Know it sounds crazy, but it works. Try it!!

So flies gross themselves out too. I would need a sandwich baggie the size of an Olympic pool.

I'm sure these people meant well. I'm also sure they did not know that visitations of flies can far exceed the scope of their solutions. Within a few days, we had flies in the garage, in the mud room, in the house. Our situation was starting to feel biblical.

Those nights, I lay in bed listening. They were still too fat, too sluggish to fly upstairs. That gave me hope. We would at least have a haven. For a while. I thought about friends who had gone into their attic and found a colony of bats hanging from the rafters. (The actual collective noun is "cloud," as in "cloud of bats." Whatever the term, it is horrible to picture.) I imagined, in a week's time, above our heads, the hum of a zillion flies in the attic. I knew it was foolish. Flies are not attic creatures. But at night, in the dark, unable to sleep, your mind wanders and comes to rest on the most elemental fears.

Bees have queens. I wondered if there was a king fly, a boss, a diabolical leader directing the invasion of our house.

At the hardware store I bought those strips of tape you unroll and hang to attract flies. I bought a couple of miles of the stuff and found it sticky and difficult to work with, subject to breezes, and simply revolting to look at. When my wife pulled in the garage, home from work, she took one look at those hanging fly strips, like unfurled rolls of film, dotted with only a few flies, and said, simply and definitively, "No."

Back at the hardware store, when the guy saw me coming, he straightened his apron and pointed me toward the hard stuff.

"Eggs," he said. "Flies lay eggs. You probably have eggs all over those garage windows."

So I hosed the windows down with poison. I would have gladly tossed buckets of the stuff. It took two or three applications and a week before we felt fly free again.

The smell of peppermint is still fresh in my nose, probably on my flip-flops, when I drive up to Midland to see my mother. She's been slipping into dementia for years now, retreating from the present into early memory. Lately the slip has become a lurch. The last time I saw her, my dad asked her if she knew who I was.

"Sure," she said. "This is Walter."

She grew up in Missaukee County, in the sticks. They had no screens, she once told me, so they hung cheesecloth in the windows during summer to let some breeze in and keep the flies out. It didn't work. Sometimes when wind agitated the cloth, she said, a curtain of flies would rise. Whenever she told me this, she gagged. Just thinking of flies made her gag.

She's sitting on the davenport with my dad when I get to the assisted living facility. They hold hands and try to talk a little.

"How are you?" I ask.

"I'm fane," she says. "Just fane."

My dad smiles. Odd word. But her tone is right. It's her.

These are their last days. They are sweet together. We try to chat, about August, about the kids moving away and the open spaces their moves create, about the nine-hour drive. My mother nods. She's far away. I suspect she's back on the farm, enjoying the fresh air. Not a fly in sight. I can only hope.

24

The Honey Room

"I'm taking a yogurt break," I tell my daughter. She's come down-stairs dressed for a friend's wedding. Six months pregnant, she's becoming abundant. Her husband is at his parents' house a few miles away. When they fly into town, out of old habit, they still go to their rooms. The yellow dress she's wearing is long, diaphanous, and, I won't tell her this, probably a mistake.

"What do you think?"

"Nice," I say.

It looks like she's dressed for a prom except for that volleyball—my eventual grandson—underneath the dress. Boy or girl, her mother and I waited to find out, game for surprise. Our daughter is a planner.

I dump walnuts in the bowl. "Your mother won't eat this," I say. "She's impervious to yogurt."

"I've got another dress upstairs. Should I try it?"

She decides for herself, rushing pregnantly up the stairs, leaving me to my snack. Yesterday my wife came home with a quart of local honey. In our mudroom we have a cupboard full of old honey, crystalized souvenir honeys she brings home from trips—clover honey, walnut honey, truffle honey. I break into the new stuff, still liquid enough to stir into my yogurt.

A bedroom door clunks shut upstairs. For twenty-five years there was a construction-paper heart taped to that door, my daughter's name written in the middle in red and blue crayon. I don't remember taking it down, but I know it's gone.

"A delicious treat," I say to no one.

My mouth is full of sweetness when they both yell up there. Yesterday I found a hairy, millepedey bug an inch long. I hope it's not one of those.

"Can you help us?" my wife yells.

She doesn't even eat honey. Come flu season, she'll put some in her tea. Otherwise, it's strictly ornamental, over there in the honey room.

The problem upstairs is zipping the dress shut. It's black and, if we can get it closed, better than the lemon parachute. The dress looks serious, formal. It takes two to make a daughter; now she's pregnant, two to get her dressed.

"Pull here."

"I am."

"Not there, here. Pull it together."

"I'm trying."

"It's too high. Let me pull it down."

"I can get it."

"Does it hurt? Is it too tight?"

"I'm huge."

"You're all right."

I admire her shoulder blades. When she was little, I told her that's where wings would grow.

"Now try."

"Hold it together."

"I am."

"Farther down."

"Ugh."

"It's all right."

"There it goes."

"Stretchy."

"Got it."

A few minutes later she's in the car, going to pick up the husband. My wife and I stand at the window, watching her back down the driveway.

"She shouldn't back up," my wife says. "She should turn the car around first. One thing your father said I agree with: never back up when you can go forward." She thinks a minute and then says: "What's that smell?"

"Yogurt," I say.

"Is she sleeping here tonight?"

"A delicious treat," I say, "with our new honey." Too good to save.

25

Bridge Failure,
Heart Attack, Fava Beans

Kacey tells me to lie down. The hospital sheets and pillowcase are blindingly white. They're not covered with paper. This is a not a cot. It's a bed with a thin mattress. My wife has trained me never to sit on a bed. Every time I did, early in our marriage, she shouted, "Street clothes!" and scared the crap out of me. After three or four times (probably ten or twenty), in order to make her stop, I stopped. When I tell Kacey this, she smiles and says, "Go ahead."

I sit on the edge of the bed, kick off my flip-flops, and lie down, looking for water spots in the acoustic tile ceiling, bathed in milky white institutional light pouring from above. She swishes around in her hospital blues, attaches electrodes to each of my feet, to my arms just above the elbow.

"Lift your shirt, please."

"How long have you been doing this?"

"Four years." She attaches a couple of electrodes to my chest. "I used to be an accountant. Then I switched careers."

"Big switch."

"I have a child with a heart condition," she says.

On the way to the hospital I heard a story on NPR about a bridge in Delaware, on the I-495 bypass. It carries ninety thousand cars a day. Its support structures are tilting. *Tilting.* The bridge can support itself, but too much weight, engineers say, like a long traffic jam, "might cause the bridge to fail." Traffic is being rerouted through downtown Wilmington, which one driver describes as "a nightmare from hell." Way worse than a nightmare from heaven. Word of the tilting bridge is traveling from Maine to Florida. Seek alternate route.

Kacey and I chat about hours and benefits, which she says are pretty good. Plus there's something new every day. New people every day. She's a people person. Once I'm hooked up, I'm expecting to be recorded for a while. I sort of want to be recorded for a while. An adult heart beats one hundred thousand times a day. Sometimes on the treadmill it occurs to me I could just fall over dead. I don't know anything about my heart. I imagine I'm improving myself through exercise, but I also picture myself crumpling mid-run, the treadmill flinging my corpse out onto the floor, where people are walking and running. Seek alternate route.

Male, sixty-one, dies thinking he's prolonging life.

There would be no such headline, I know. Mine would be an anonymous, perfunctory death. I also know there would be no quotation from my wife, because she would never talk to the media. But if there were a quotation, she would probably say I seemed healthy enough. "We thought his heart was fine." After all, I had survived her scaring the living crap out of me ten or twenty times.

Kacey touches a button, and it's done. Just like that.

"That's all?"

She starts peeling off electrodes. "That's it."

"How's it look?"

She glances at the display. So do I.

"I'm a tech," she says. "I'm supposed to wait for a cardiologist." She points at waves, lines, and blips. There are numbers. She should be good with numbers. "Looks excellent," she says.

Later that day I drive to a local market looking for fava beans. They're in season, though these days, it could be argued, given modern infrastructure, everything is in season all the time. You live in Michigan and want a Bartlett pear in January? No problem. Mango, kiwi, kumquat, rambutan, whatever you want, they got it, or at least a durable, tasteless facsimile of it. This modern achievement falls into the nightmare from heaven category. For some reason, fava only come in early summer and last only a few weeks. I've made a commitment to them.

Half a mile before I reach the store, I see a runner on the sidewalk. She's wearing a white top and navy blue shorts. It is within her powers, I'm sure, to slow traffic approaching her from behind. A minute later, getting out of my car, I see her again, running through the store parking lot, which seems odd. Maybe there's sidewalk repair going on; she's taken an alternate route. I pause as she runs by and then pause a few seconds more.

The fava beans are in. They're packaged on brown Styrofoam trays, sealed in plastic wrap, which means I can't touch them, can't gauge their freshness. A sign says "organic." Subtext: better for you. Sub-subtext: double the price. There's another market near my next stop that might have them for less money, piles of them in a basket so you can palpate the pods, counting the beans within, testing their firmness the way I imagine a physician feels for tumors.

On the way to the next store I see the runner in the blue shorts ahead. I pull alongside her and stop at an intersection as she too slows and stops. She bends, stretching, touching her toes, then uprights herself. She does a few lateral stretches, turning left and right on her axis, then begins running slowly in place. Her perfection is a reminder: things may be gradually falling apart, but new is also a permanent condition. It's a sunny day. For the time being my heart is doing its job.

And I'm shopping for this year's fava beans.

26

Monkey, Nail Biting, Jesus

I just wish he didn't sit down there in front.

I tell my wife this early one Monday morning. We're at the breakfast table. I'm making her cappuccino while she reads about Naples. The one in Italy. She moves around the boot, reading histories of the regions. She has just come inland from Sicily.

"Don't look at him," she says.

We're discussing a kid who grooms himself during church service. I don't mean the primping kind of grooming, because he wants to look nice. Looking nice is not on his agenda. This is more of a creatural thing. As soon as he sits down, he goes to work on his fingernails, scraping crud out from under them. He then raises his fingers to his face, examines the stuff, and judging it good, eats it. After nails he moves to his hair, which is curly, sandy in color, and the source of additional morsels. He digs and scratches at his scalp, scrutinizes and ingests the harvest. Whatever grows on him and is sloughed off his person is on the menu. "Lift up your hearts," the priest says. The kid is eating himself. Next to him sit a mother, a sister or two. They seem oblivious.

I hand my wife a coffee cup. "He eats himself," I say.

She takes a sip. "He's a kid."

"Still," I say, "there's a time and place."

She reads for a minute and then looks up from her book. "The King of Naples was married to the sister of Marie Antoinette."

I go to the fridge. Every morning I cut fruits and vegetables into the blender for a smoothie. My wife sometimes calls it a "frappé," which I love. She's never tried to make a Catholic of me, which I also love. Most days I'm more spectator than believer.

I tell her there's a name for what the kid does.

"She was Maria Carolina of Austria."

"Autosarcophagy," I say. "The act of eating yourself. And he's not little. He must be ten or twelve."

"He's probably bored. Doesn't your mind wander?"

Does it ever. Generally, I admit, it wanders to pleasures of the flesh. We're supposed to do that. *Let us call to mind our sins.* I require no invitation.

When I was a kid my father made deliveries at a farm north of town. It was a traditional farm—tractors, a barn, cows and pigs—except for the monkey.

The monkey was a thin, dusty thing, the size of a poodle. It lived in a repurposed dog pen. When we pulled in the driveway and stopped next to the gas tank we were there to fill, my brother and I hopped out of the truck right next to the monkey. It amused my father, I think, how excited we got about seeing a monkey. He would tell us a day or so ahead: "I'll be at Paul Hafer's on Thursday." And we would prepare to see this exotic creature. It had a chain around its neck. It usually sat on the roof of the doghouse with a preoccupied look on its face. It picked at its fur with nimble fingers, finding fleas and lice, which naturally it ate.

We begged our father for a monkey. It would make a great pet, we argued.

We were told in no uncertain terms that it would never happen and that we should not under any circumstances try to touch it.

Deep down, I know my father hated that monkey, its nervous eyes, its high-pitched chatter, its terrible pink behind that it repeatedly flashed at us.

Years later, my wife invoked the theory of evolution. My father saw the monkey as a distant relative. He identified with it.

This, I told her, was pure bunk.

"Saw himself," she insisted, "in the monkey."

"More likely he just hated the smell."

Who knows? Maybe she was right. And maybe I see myself in the kid in church who eats himself.

And identify with him.

I am now, and have always been, a nail biter. Nail biting is an infantile oral fixation, I readily admit, like thumb-sucking. It is also reckless and daft, importing filth and bacteria into my system. I might as well lick doorknobs and suck nickels.

It is also a source of pleasure and pain.

I practice fingernail husbandry. Nails are a renewable resource, but, you know, there is a season. Left ring finger should be ready for biting in a day or two. Excellent yield from right pointer and thumb last week. What constitutes a mature, ripe, and ready nail? It's personal. For me, it's neither too brittle nor too soft. Timing is everything.

Also, I like a nice, clean arc, even in density and thickness across the width of the nail, tapered at the edges. I try, not always successfully, not to overbite.

The sight of ravaged nails, gnawed down to their moons, their cuticles red and ragged, is heartrending. Through husbandry and restraint, I usually manage to avoid this massacre. Eyes are the window of the soul; fingernails also tell us plenty. Salinger comes to mind, his description of the headmaster's insecure daughter in *Catcher in the Rye*—"Her nails were all bitten down and bleedy-looking"—and poor, traumatized Esmé: "She placed her fingers flat on the table edge, like someone at a seance, then, almost instantly, closed her hands—her nails were bitten down to the quick."

When I'm sitting in a meeting or stopped at an intersection and I see someone gnawing on their fingertips with that urgency, that uncontrollable driven look, I feel revolted and chastened. *Don't do that*, I tell myself. *Down, boy*, I think, especially when the urge arises in public. Sometimes I cross over, however, to the other side. On one finger on my right hand, I have a situation. It's the middle one, the "finger" finger. I trim it by nibble with the utmost care. But I've bitten it wrong too many times. I've bitten it for too long, too hungrily. The nail now grows to a certain length, and then it splits, and the cuticle gets tattered and erupts. It hurts. I mean it *hurts*. At times a crusty tissue forms on the cuticle, which my daughter and wife refer to as a fungus.

"Ugh," my daughter says, "you got that fungus."

It is not a fungus.

"It's green," my wife says. "A green fungus."

It is not a fungus.

They take turns hectoring me about it.

"Don't touch me with that."

"You don't put that in your mouth, do you?"

I won't. I don't.

I do.

"Jesus Christ, don't bite your nails." She must have said that. When God became a man, it was Mary who made him a nice boy.

If the mother of God got after him about His nails, it was good advice. Who would throw away everything and follow someone whose nails were bitten down and bleedy-looking? It would have pushed Thomas over the edge and maybe a few of the others. But would you blame Jesus for being just a little bit nervous? He had a lot on His mind.

Happy are those who are called to His supper.

When she was a kid in Italy, my wife says she often walked down the street to the convent and visited the old nuns. They ran the *asilo*, the preschool program. She was an alum. They also made host, mixing the dough and letting it dry in thin sheets. These sheets were then slid into a mechanism, a die they used to stamp out the perfectly round wafers that would be consecrated and served at Communion. If she was good, the nuns let her eat the leftovers. She remembers stuffing scraps of it into her mouth, handfuls of it, gorging herself on host until one of the sisters swept her back out onto the street.

I think of this gobbling one morning in church.

Row by row, front to back, in the call to Communion people process down the aisle. Heads bowed, hands folded in front of them or clasped behind their backs or idle at their sides, they wait for a little nibble of Christ, for a sip of wine, "fruit of the vine and work of human hands."

I fall in line behind my wife.

When it's my turn, I take the host in my hands and say "Amen." I place the wafer in my mouth and turn to the right.

There he is, the little manimal, an alternative reminder of our source.

This morning he is slumped over the pew in front of him, resting his head on his arm. He looks full, satisfied, possibly even asleep. Back in our pew, my wife kneels, closes her eyes. It'll be a few minutes before we can go. I sit forward in a kneelish posture, let my mind wander, and have a look around. Eventually I come back to the kid. He's awake and seems to be about his business. When he inserts a finger into his mouth, I can guess what he's doing. He's had Communion. Savior is stuck to the roof of his mouth, and he's trying to loosen it.

The same thing happens to me. It's an odd sensation, sort of like having a pebble in your shoe. I work at it and work at it with my tongue. Sometimes it takes forever.

27

Cardio, Lightbulbs, and a Funeral

The day of the funeral I'm on the treadmill at the senior center.

A guy named Gordon I haven't seen in a while stops next to me and points. I shake my head, *What?* He points again. So: I guess my limp is noticeable. I took a minor tumble on some stairs, more sprawl than fall.

I'd rather not go into it right now. I'm listening to Ray Charles sing "Oh, what a beautiful morning" on my headset and watching Kelly Ripa and Michael Strahan on one of the four TVs hung on the wall. But Gordon stands there, smiling. I pause the Ray, pop out an earbud.

"You hurt?" he says.

"Not much." I dial down the speed and nod hello. "Where you been?"

"On a yacht," he says. "What happened?"

Gordon is a junior senior. His hair is all white. He's retired, not yet sixty, and reminds me of the Pillsbury Doughboy. The two years I've worked out at the senior center, I'll see Gordon three days a week every week for a stretch. Then he'll be gone for weeks at a time. He is swift on the elliptical and then swiftly done and gone upstairs for coffee and networking. I glance back at the TV. It's confetti time on

Kelly and Michael. Three days a week I watch the silent confetti-drop. It's goofy, but everyone in the studio loves it. I guess I do too.

I tell him I took a little fall down some stairs. There's a pause. I'm still walking, he's standing by. "So," I say. "A yacht."

"There's no such thing as a little fall," he says.

"Whereabouts, Caribbean?"

"Not this time," he says. "Up in the North Channel. With Don." Don is one of the senior seniors. He says he's too old for exercise equipment. He wears big shoes and sleds a few laps around the tiny indoor track before stopping for a long coffee. He does a couple of cruises a year. Gordon must be first mate.

"Every afternoon," he says, "cocktail hour on the flying bridge, some cool jazz. It was sweet."

"Must be some yacht."

He considers his answer, smiles, and says, "Not that big."

I start to say there's no such thing as a small yacht but think otherwise. I kind of want to get back to Ray Charles. I point to the TV and ask what he thinks of Kelly Ripa's hair. It's new, a Frenchy-looking bob. I don't think she likes it. She touches it a lot.

Gordon glances at the TV, then back at me, like, *Are you joking?*

Later that morning I squeeze in a trip to Home Depot, looking for lightbulbs and superglue.

A few days ago my wife called to me from the basement. She said the stairway lights were out, one at the top, one at the bottom. That stairway goes down three steps to a landing and then makes a right turn to go down the rest of the way, thirteen steps in all, all carpeted. I stood on a toppish step; she was downstairs. We flipped switches and talked. It was definitely dark. It turned out I didn't know what step I was on. When I went to set my foot on the landing, it wasn't quite there, and suddenly I went down in a pile of twisted and stretched muscle, bone, and fat.

"I'm okay," I said to my wife. It was a tentative assessment, kind of a lie. I hurt like hell.

"Are you sure?"

"Probably," I told her. I just didn't feel like moving yet.

Falls run in the family. In his old age my father stepped off a ladder and crashed onto the cement floor in the garage. He limped for a month. When she was seventy my mother-in-law misjudged a stair step in our house, fell, and broke her ankle. One night my father-in-law woke up and walked the length of his house in the dark to the bathroom, the one he used over by the garage, the one next to the door to the basement. He opened the wrong door and stepped into the dark stairway. There was no landing to abbreviate his fall. He tumbled straight down all thirteen stairs. Somehow, he was not hurt.

Thirteen. That should tell us something.

For some time now whenever I carry a case of wine to the basement, I imagine myself slipping and falling. Put carpet on stairs, you're tempting fate. In this imagined fall my arms fly up, I launch the case of wine into the air, and bottles fly and fall, breaking and spilling. When I roll into the glassy, winey mess at the bottom of the stairs, I cut my throat. Cheers.

In the aisles of Home Depot I decide to look for the long-lasting bulbs. Bulb technology, it turns out, is taking giant, if confusing, steps forward. Really, it's a stampede. There's incandescent, halogen, fluorescent, compact fluorescent, and LED. Check for lumens, watts, kelvin value, for soft light, hard light, dimables, and warm-up time. Then there's savings per year, calculated to the penny, and year life. It's kind of like shopping for French wine. The light steward I eventually talk to holds out a package of bulbs, recommends LED.

"How long will they last?" I ask.

He looks at me and smiles. "You'll probably never have to buy bulbs again." It's an innocent remark. In my lifetime, he means. He sees something in my facial expression, intimations of my imminent demise, and offers a sheepish apology.

On the way to the funeral my wife says, "They're not supposed to die before us."

No, they're not.

He was fifty. He was big. He had a mountain-man beard and a soft voice. He had light in his eyes and a smile that made you want to love him. At the funeral we stand in the church vestibule for half an hour, a visitation that begins in soft murmuring and mournful glances and rises to a din of conversation and laughter so loud the funeral director can't hush us up and herd us into the church. There's a balm in that din, an affirmation. But still, the man is gone.

We file in, find seats in pews, and wait. Whoever made this church understood light. The floor and walls and ceiling are all white. There's stained glass, but it's stained glass lite. The afternoon sunlight pouring in has a kind of echo. Maybe it helps. While we wait, the pianist plays in minor keys, slowly, a lot of sostenuto. Maybe that helps too. I remark to my wife: above the altar, the wheel chandelier hanging from the ceiling. When she looks, I whisper, "A little lower, it could be a pot rack." She wags a finger: keep quiet. Way off to the left, behind the organ, is a huge set of drums worthy of Ginger Baker and a pile of amplifiers for playing God rock. The horror.

Then the pianist shifts to a major key. We stand.

Then come the family, the casket, words.

Outside afterward, we stand facing the hearse, arguably the worst time. One church bell begins to toll. I hope they're doing it on purpose. "*If a clod be washed away by the sea*," I think. We are the less.

Lying in bed that night I find my wife's hand and remember: superglue. It's for a ceramic lemon that she bought in Sicily and that I broke a few weeks ago. I plan to fix it. Two or three pieces, clean breakage. It will be almost good as new. We lie there, drifting toward sleep. Drifting, I think about lemons and glue, and carpet on a well-lit stairway, about my limp to wellness on the treadmill, about a yacht anchored in the North Channel, floating in the dark, a couple of staterooms lit by a few tiny lights, and people having drinks, feeling lucky.

28

The Rule of One

Apply pressure and elevate.

I know that's how you stop bleeding. But this is my nose. I just cut it shaving. A careless flick of the razor and I caught the wing of my right nostril. The gore, the gore. I don't know how to elevate my nose.

"You ready?" my wife yells from downstairs.

Since when is she ready before me? We're going for an R and R dinner tonight. That's Rachel and Ron, our friends we told where to go in Italy. They went, they're back, we've seen some pictures online. They're going to tell us about it. And now I've got this bleeding nostril.

"Almost." I press a handful of toilet paper to the wound.

"If we leave early we can swing by Newton and look at trees."

Some weeks ago we planted three cherry trees in the yard. Overnight they were denuded of leaves by deer. In crisis mode we set out deer repellent, a particulate poured into leftover pantyhose and hung from the branches. Not attractive, which I guess is the point if you're a deer. Not attractive if you're a human either, which doesn't matter to my wife. Such is her commitment to trees, while I am Darwinian.

I yell okay. But this thing is not okay. If it would just clot. Stick a piece of toilet paper on it, usually it clots. Not this time.

"Let's get some of that spray," she yells up to me. Another repellent, one you spray on the tree. It's Off for deer. I hear on the steps she's coming up.

She pushes through the door into the bathroom, sees the sink full of bloody tissues. "Hey, what?"

"I cut myself."

"I can see that. Geez, it's bloody. Did you try a Band-Aid? Did you stick a piece of toilet paper on it? Did you apply pressure?"

"All those things."

"How about ice?"

"That's for swelling."

"Still."

"Swelling, bleeding, not the same thing."

She opens a door of the vanity. "Gauze."

I tell her first we have to stop the bleeding.

"Should we go to emergency? Lemme see that." I lift the toilet paper from my sliced nostril. In the mirror I see a red ribbon of blood trickle down my lip. It's just like TV.

"Ew," she says.

"Ow," I say. It really hurts.

"What about one of those things?"

A butterfly stitch, I think she means. "That might work," I say.

On the way to the drugstore we talk about replacement trees, in case our cherry trees pass away. How about a ginkgo tree? How about a red bud? We could plant another honey locust. Maybe deer prey on fruit trees.

"All the little trees are dying," she says. That old crab apple won't last much longer. Two bad winters in a row.

I hold tissue to my nose, which continues to seep blood. I've got more tissues in my pockets, just in case. She says she hopes we're not too late for dinner.

The pharmacist, when we ask first aid advice, wants to see the cut. I show him and he says he doesn't think a butterfly stitch will work, we're welcome to try, but he recommends an antihemorrhagic. "Your nose is wet where the stitch should adhere," he says. "A butterfly stitch will come loose."

"His nose is always wet," my wife says. "He's like a beagle."

The pharmacist points at my nose. "Jack Nicholson."

"What?"

"*Chinatown?* The movie? He's J. J. Gittes. And Faye Dunaway is . . . someone. Wonderful film. Water rights, skullduggery. Very up to date all of a sudden, wouldn't you say?" He squints a little, peers at my nose, considers it. He has a reddish nose. He's balding on top and has longish gray hair, long enough to cover his ears. He's obviously worn the white coat for quite a while. "Roman Polanski," he says, "wielding a switchblade. I believe the Nicholson nose required stitches."

"Gittes," I say.

He nods.

"He cut himself shaving," my wife explains, implying, I guess, that there is no skullduggery. "Will he need stitches?"

He points us to aisle five. Tells us styptic pencil is our best bet.

I read the package out loud in the car: "Anhydrous aluminum sulfate." So that's what it is.

"Do it."

"A vasoconstrictor," I say. "This stuff hurts."

"Doesn't it hurt already? You're bleeding. Do it. Shouldn't you try it?"

I lean forward, strain to see my nose in the rearview mirror. I'll do it when we get to Rachel and Ron's, I tell her. It might be messy.

Rachel and Ron have wine and cheese, fresh figs, and fennel ready in their recently redone kitchen. It's all white: cupboards, cabinets, countertops, blindingly white and beautiful.

"Let's nosh. Let's have some Frascati," Rachel says. "I can drink this stuff like Fresca. I only want Frascati now."

"We say 'antipasto,'" Ron says. "We're so Italian."

"Rome was beautiful. The artichokes, the fountains."

"It was hot. They drink wine at 10:00 a.m."

"What's wrong with your nose? Good God!"

"He cut himself shaving."

"You forget it's a razor in your hand. You get so casual. It's like scratching your eyebrow with the barrel of a gun."

"Wait, you still use a razor? Aren't you electric?"

"He's got no visible beard."

"I just love figs. Figs and Frascati."

"I have facial hair. It's transparent."

"And gray."

"Transparent and gray. Could I use your bathroom? I need to fix myself up."

The styptic pencil reminds me of a tube of lipstick: white lipstick, cold fire. I run it under the cold water faucet and daub my nostril. It burns, holy cow it burns so much my right eye tears up. "You okay?" Ron yells from the kitchen. I hear wine glasses, a cork popped from another bottle. They're touching on subjects: Florence and the Baptistery doors, Rome and the Romans, Caravaggio, riding in taxis. I touch the cut again, press tissue against it, and wait. No go. Vasoconstrictor, my ass. Pressure on, pressure off, a few more styptic burns, until finally there's a milky film of anhydrous aluminum sulfate up and down the right side of my nose.

"Everything all right?"

"Looks like you were snorting in there."

"Good for now."

"You need to be more careful. How on earth do you cut your nose? If you can cut your nose, you can cut your throat."

"Yum, figs."

"This woman in our group, everywhere we go in Rome she's like, 'This is nice, but it's hard to beat Piazza della Senorita.' Did she not say that, Ron?"

"She did say that. But I think it was just for the fun."

"And every night, she orders that tomato mozzarella salad and calls it a 'Caprice,' like the Chevy car? 'Um, I'll have the Caprice.' The waiter, waitress, they roll their eyes and say "cah-PRAY-zay." Next night it's Caprice all over again."

"You say that very well."

"Caprese."

"Bingo."

"Thanks. You were right, though. We hung with the tour guide only for a little while. Then, see ya."

"A lot of old people."

"So many old people."

"But the cutest couple. Tell them about the cutest couple, Ray."

"How about another glass of wine? One for the nose?"

"Nope. Rule of one."

"They've been married forty years. Tony and Diane. Every trip they take, they find one of those photo booths, like in shopping centers, remember those things when you were a kid? You sit on these stools and mug for the camera and get a strip of black and white pictures. They have forty or fifty of those things. Every trip they take."

"Romantic."

"Cute."

"They were like kids."

"They were like newlyweds. All over each other. They made the Italians blush."

"So, about the rule of one."

"It's his new thing."

"One glass of wine. One dish of pasta. One potato, one piece of meat, one piece of cake. Take what you want. Just take one."

"Why would you do such a thing?"

"So, like, one glass of Frascati, one glass of Sauvignon Blanc? One Merlot? I'll just keep opening bottles."

"Nope. One is one."

"It's the loneliest number."

My wife taps the side of her nose. "You're bleeding again."

"You might need a stitch."

"I think we should move to the dinner table."

A couple swipes of the styptic pencil is all it takes. I stand in front of the mirror looking at my old face while Rachel and Ron put dinner on the table. Rachel's talking about Florence, a pasta they ate with pear sauce and asparagus tips. She tries to say the pasta name. "Fiocchetti," my wife says. "Was that it?" She says it two or three times, calling attention to the double consonants. Rachel repeats. I turn my head to the left, the better to see my nostril. So this is my old face. So many wrinkles. One day years ago I was driving west. It was early evening. Stopped at a light, I looked in the mirror and saw, for the first time, all this gray over my temples. What the hell? Tonight I take in my drooping eyelids, the long, deepening furrows in my cheeks. The skin in my neck is beginning to look slack.

"You're back."

"Chianti. Let's open that Chianti now."

"I cauterized myself."

"It better work this time. You bleed again we're going to emergency."

"I was up late a few nights ago. *Rambo* was on TV."

"Ron, please, don't talk about *Rambo* at the dinner table."

"It's the third movie. Rambo goes to Afghanistan, where he fights with the Mujahedin. Those were the days when the people who want to kill us today were sort of our friends. So Rambo and the Mujahedin are fighting the Soviets, and Rambo gets wounded."

"He just likes to say 'Mujahedin.'"

"Three *Rambo*s. Where is the rule of one when you need it?"

"He's got this shrapnel in his side that he pulls out, and blood comes oozing from the wound, kind of like your nose. What does Rambo do? He takes the gunpowder out of a bullet and pours it in the wound and lights it. He lights it, with a little torch. There's this explosion, and flames and smoke shoot out both sides of the wound. Rambo, he just takes it."

"That's what I just did. You must have smelled the smoke."

"Poor Rambo, he's so dim."

"All he knows is rage."

"And vengeance."

"Everything else is inchoate."

"Meaning?"

"I'm not quite sure."

"Then why say it?"

"No. Inchoate, you're not quite sure, kind of muddled."

"Rambo, man of muddle."

"That's how Rambo stops the bleeding."

"All right, I'll have one more glass, just because it's Chianti."

"Tony and Diane, that couple on our trip, told us a sad story, about their dog that died. It got to be old and infirm, deaf and disoriented. It would wander into a closet and couldn't find its way out."

"Poor thing."

"The car, Ray."

"Yes, the car. The dog loved to go for rides. Just loved it. One day it sort of fell out an open car window. Tony turned, Diane swerved, I don't remember. The dog tumbled out the window at thirty-five miles per hour."

"Onto a grassy shoulder."

"It was a grassy shoulder. They stressed that. And the dog was okay, but not. It walked and ran fine, but mentally it started slipping."

"Dogs get dementia."

"Canine Alzheimer's."

"Finally they had it put down."

"A terrible expression. Don't say that, Ray."

"And they decided to have the dog preserved."

"Stuffed?"

"Yes!"

"'Our one and only dog,' Diane said. 'We couldn't bear to part with it.'"

"One is the loneliest number."

"What do you do with a stuffed dog? Keep it on the hearth, with its little dog dish next to it?"

"I wonder if you could do that with humans? Stuff Nana and keep her in the family room."

"What about Lenin? What about Mao? They're stuffed. And that guy in Venezuela?"

"They're lying down. They're dead. Stand Nana up. Make her lifelike."

"Wouldn't you want to remember the dog in its youth? Its most lively and frisky state? Rather than, 'There's old Fido, right after he got lost in the closet.'"

"Something tells me he may end up in the closet."

"Probably Nana, if she had any say-so, would not want to be preserved the way she looked on her final day."

"Where would we put your mother, Ray?"

"There's more. They get the dog home, and it's doing something that bothers them. Really bothers them. The dog is standing there with one paw raised. You know how dogs strike that funny pose?"

"Interrogative."

"Quit it."

"'It never did that in real life,' Tony said. 'The dog was brimming with confidence. It threw caution to the wind.'"

"Canine carpe diem."

"'Brimming with confidence?' He said that?"

"More or less."

"Probably for the taxidermist, it was an opportunity. You can imagine him, a craftsman, thinking, 'I'll make this dog stand on its own three feet, with one foot raised, expressing personality.'"

"An interrogative pose."

"More like, WTF?"

"Wouldn't they have a pre-preservation conference with the taxidermist to iron out those details?"

"Okay, one more glass. Then that's it."

"See how strong he is?"

"See how silly it is to live by principles?"

"It's very good Chianti. Or what is it now?"

"You're having one glass of Barbaresco."

"You say that very well. Barbaresco and Mujahedin."

"I'm picturing that old dog."

"Holding its WTF pose, for all of eternity."

"God, that's a long time."

"In the Rapture, you know, the virtuous are sucked up into heaven, for all of eternity. Not just your spirit, but your body too."

"There's a good reason you should stop at one glass."

"It's in the Bible. Body and soul."

"Our tribe has a different mythology, don't we, Ray? Don't we just die?"

"The living and the dead, bodied and re-embodied, off to heaven they go."

"I think we just die."

"What I want to know is, which body goes to heaven? Take Nana. Is she raptured away in her old, decrepit body—liver spots, mustache, loss of bone density, half-blind? Or can she say, you know, 'Make me twenty-one'? 'I'd like to be thirty-five?'"

"You should have seen Rach at eighteen."

"Thank you, Ray."

"If I went tonight, would I have this Jack Nicholson nose for all of eternity?"

"What?"

"And Diane and Tony's dog, lost in heaven's closets, looking for its dog dish?"

"Jack Nicholson nose?"

"Don't ask. He's exceeded his one-glass limit. We better say good night."

It's a long good-bye. Global warming, the rising of the lakes, why can't they build a decent road where we live. Now the Roman road system was something else, my wife reminds us, and we give three cheers for the Appian Way. Next time, how about some Italian lessons? How do you say "next time" in Italian?

Back home, lying in bed, we talk about trees.

"Right now the deer could be out there," my wife says, "finishing off our cherry trees."

Tomorrow we'll definitely go to Newton. We'll buy deer Off. We'll look at some replacement trees. She suggests rose of Sharon, I suggest baobab. "There's a baobab tree in Africa, I tell her, that's six thousand years old." How about one of those? That's a tree with thick skin. She gets up and finds a towel to cover my pillow, says I might bleed in the middle of the night. I would like to guarantee her that I won't.

29

Water Me

Some years ago my wife and I had lunch at Scoma's in Sausalito.
While we ate, the waiter told us his immigration story—transplanted
from Italy to Philadelphia, then Las Vegas, now San Francisco.
There was good money in restaurant work, he said. He wanted to
put away as much as he could, then move back to Puglia. Our two
kids were supposed to be outside on the restaurant deck overlook-
ing the bay. Except my daughter, ten at the time, was now pulling
on my sleeve.

"He's trapped," she said.

"Trapped where?" I said. "Is he okay?"

She covered her mouth, barely containing her delight. "His head
is stuck in the fence."

"The fence!" the waiter said.

She led us outside to her brother. Our five-year-old had pushed
his head through the rails on the wrought iron deck fence to see
better and was now staring down into a bank of swaying seaweed,
holding the bars like a prisoner, calm, a little sheepish.

The waiter said he'd run and get some olive oil.

"What, to oil his head?"

"Well, the poor kid."

"Wait," I said. "If he got his head in there, we ought to be able to get it out." After lunch we were going to Muir Woods. I pictured loading an oily child into the rental car and then dragging him around the redwoods.

The trick was all in the ears. With a little pressing and folding, he popped out, born again, blinking, but okay.

"Would you like a glass of water?" the waiter asked.

"Huh?" the boy said. "Water?"

"Huh?" I said.

What is it with Italians and water? Recently, walking around a no-traffic zone in Rimini, I heard what could only be described as a heavy splat. I turned and saw that a late middle-aged woman, somewhat on the heavy side, had tripped and fallen face-first to the pavement. A man nearby rushed to her side, helped her sit up, and asked if she would like a glass of water. She said she was okay. Seconds later a store clerk who had seen the fall ran outside and told her she should go file a complaint with the city. Then *she* asked the woman if she would like a glass of water. The woman said she was okay, but they insisted on getting her to take a drink. The clerk ran back into the store and a few seconds later came out with a plastic water bottle and a small plastic cup.

To Italians, sometimes water is more than just water. It soothes a stuck head and a smashed face. At a local Italian market where I shop here in Detroit, I used to see an old gentleman buying cases of San Benedetto bottled water. "It's good for the kidneys," he explained one day in the parking lot, "and keeps the prostate from heating up." Water can do that?

There is a long tradition in Europe of people "taking the waters" for their health benefits. The Italians refer to it as "the cure." The 1828 edition of *London Universal Dictionary of Science, Art, Literature, and Practical Mechanics* lists close to six hundred sites in Europe offering mineral waters with health benefits. There is a distinct British bias. Here is one entry, for Harrowgate, in Yorkshire: "Discovered in 1571 by captain [*sic*] Slingsby; found to contain sulfur, muriate of soda, and purging salt; destroys worms; is praised in scurvy, scrofula, palsy, and chiefly in cutaneous hemorrhages." And here is the reference, from the *Universal Dictionary*, to Italy: "Contains many sulfurous and warm springs, of little note."

Tell the Italians that. San Pellegrino Terme was already a thing in the thirteenth century. Castrocaro was a destination for the Romans. They called it "Salsubium" (a place rich in waters). A few years ago my wife took me to Castrocaro. We soaked in water, waded in it, inhaled it in its steam state, dunked in cold baths of it, and, of course, drank some. Neither of us has since been troubled by scurvy or scrofula. Nor have I broken any bones. And I think I sing better. Amazing water. Just the names of some bottled waters in Italy smack of the miraculous: Fonte Santafiore, Acqua della Madonna, Acqua Santa Chianciano, Acqua dell Cardinale, San Fautino, San Giorgio, San Pelligrino, Santa Vittoria, Sergente Angelica.

The first time I went to Italy, a few months after I was married, I was told not to drink the tap water. While we were settling into the family apartment, my wife's uncle carried in a few cases of bottled water. I pointed at the tap in the kitchen sink. What about that? "No one drinks that," he said. This was before bottled water had become a common consumer product in the United States. The way I was raised, if you were thirsty, you went to the tap. That was my aquatic orientation. It was an August visit to Italy, and it was hot. There was no AC. For ten days, everywhere we went, we were on the bottle.

One afternoon, I made a water run with the uncle to the spring called Fonte Sacramora. We loaded cases of empty glass bottles into the trunk of his car and drove thirty minutes to Viserba, next to the sea. We waited in line. "Acqua buona," he said.

And miraculous, I learned.

Legend has it, when Saint Julian was martyred in 305, he was sewed inside a sack full of scorpions and vipers and tossed in the sea. His body came ashore in Alexandria and was buried in Antioch, where he remained until around the year 950, when his tomb traveled, by water, across the Mediterranean, up the Adriatic, and came ashore in Viserba. On the spot it came ashore there sprang a spring. That's some water.

It was free, it tasted good, but it wasn't tap water.

These days I'm observing the rule of one—one glass of wine with meals and a lot of water. I take ice water with meals. Between meals I measure consumption in swallows, not in glasses, cupping my hand under the water streaming from the kitchen faucet and slupping down twelve swallows. Twelve swallows how many times a day? On a good day, every time I pee, I then go the kitchen and drink. That's my system: pee, drink; drink, pee. More swallowing, more frequent peeing. More frequent peeing, more swallowing. I know it's indelicate, but: what gorgeous pee. A crystal clear, faintly greenish rushing cataract.

I'm operating on the assumption that a lot of water is good for me. I know it's possible to kill yourself drinking water, but I'm careful. And the health benefits are legion. Water aids in mental concentration, energizes muscles, is good for your skin, and flushes toxins from your body (witness my pee). The eight-glasses-of-water rule? Probably bunk. A 1945 publication by the National Food Nutrition Board recommended two and a half liters of water daily, which is about eight eight-ounce glasses of water. Since then eight has been the magic number. A more common sense approach: drink when you're thirsty. My approach—well, enough about that.

Ice water, on the other hand, raises questions. According to a California State Science Fair project in 2008, drinking ice water with a meal is not good. Says the researcher: "Drinking cold water with your meal is harmful for your health. It delays the process of emulsification of fat because it solidifies it. This causes the fat to cling to the villi for a longer time, which prevents other important nutrients from being absorbed." I totally forgot about my villi. This warning about ice water is fairly common. Dr. Stephen Sinatra, an integrative cardiologist, also cautions against ice water with food, referring to the resulting imbalance between *agni* (Sanskrit for digestive fire) and *ama* (Sanskrit for toxins).

I'll have problems with ice water the next time I'm in Italy. For one thing, there's never enough ice. Ask for ice in a restaurant, they bring you a saucer with a couple of ice cubes the size of dice. The typical American looks for ice on a glacial scale. Then there's the Italian belief, I'm not sure how widely held, that ice water is bad for you. The uncle who took me to Sacramora always said, "Acqua fredda fa male alla pancia." "Cold water gives you a stomachache." In addition to snuffing out your digestive fire and freezing your intestinal villi.

In a few days my wife and I are going back to San Francisco. To prepare for the trip, I've been reading up on restaurants. I'm expecting to see this sign: *Water served on request.* Meaning tap water. I'm sure there's all the bottled water you want. Given my rule of one, and the attendant desire to drink gallons of tap water, I'm a little nervous. How bad is the water situation out there? A few weeks ago Tom Selleck was accused of stealing water for his fifty-acre avocado ranch. The charge turned out to be bogus, but the fact that it was made is an indicator of water pressure.

Unfortunately, I recently watched *Dawn of the Planet of the Apes* on television. I can't think of Muir Woods now without seeing apes in the trees and, across the bay in San Francisco, a militarized dystopia. What kind of civilization would we have if there were a severe, long-term water shortage? You imagine something akin to the one represented in that ape movie: one segment of the population with a sufficient water supply (apes, as it were, who have ready access to water from the reservoir), another segment on the verge of violence and extinction, holding mayhem at bay only as long as the bottled water lasts.

30

Feathers

"Help me with the *piumino*," she says.

My wife is holding an armful of duvet cover, still warm from the dryer. We're going to stuff the duvet (*piumino* in Italian) into the cover, an ordeal that makes me long for the simple days of my youth, when bedding consisted of flat sheet, blanket, and bedspread.

Ordinarily I like things ending in -*ino* and -*ini*, a diminutive Italian suffix that confers cuteness on just about anything. Even a turd—*stronzino*—becomes adorable in the Italian diminutive. I do not love the piumino.

"Must I?"

"Yes, you must."

The problem is fit. We have an oversize cover. It's too long and too wide—the duvet floats around inside the cover like a slippery manta ray as we pinch it, feeling around for edges, trying to trap the duvet while it is approximately centered. It is a doomed effort, which means eventually either the lower or upper region of our bed will have lots of duvet, capable of achieving incubation-level temperatures.

"I hate this thing," I say.

"It's easier." She's standing on a chair at the foot of the bed, getting ready to fluff the duvet. "You center it, you poof it, and you're done," she says.

"You're standing on a chair to make the bed. That's easy?"

"Yes."

"I hate this thing."

She fluffs the duvet, parachuting it to the mattress. It takes three or four poofs to get the job done. She climbs down from the chair, says it looks nice. She likes it.

Does she ever. She likes it so much she even leaves it on our bed in the summer. All summer I toss the thing off me all night long. All night she tosses it back on. Some mornings I wake up feeling like poached sole.

I was not yet out of primary school when my mother taught me how to make a bed. I learned to execute hospital corners on both the top sheet and blanket and then smooth a bedspread over the whole, finishing with a crisp tuck under the pillow. Comfort then was measured in foot-pounds of blanket weight you felt piled on in the winter, the heavier the better. If you had feathers, they were in your pillow.

The dispute comes down to your feather orientation: feathers on the bottom or feathers on top.

History suggests humans originally, and through much of recorded time, preferred feathers on the bottom. Feather beds date back to the fourteenth century, though as a rarity, primarily comforting the well-to-do. By the nineteenth century, however, they were more common. The feather "tick" also made its appearance at this time. The tick was essentially a linen or cotton bag full of feathers (fifty pounds of feathers!), which was then laid over a mattress. You would lie on the tick, not pull the tick over you. God was in his heaven, and all the feathers were beneath us.

Not, evidently, on the continent, where the duvet was becoming a thing, popularizing the feathers-on-top orientation. The term "duvet," meaning "down," dates back to eighteenth-century French. Samuel Johnson, in 1759, refers with skepticism to an advertisement for duvets, noting, "Promise, large promise, is the soul of an advertisement," and citing, as an example, "'duvets for bed-coverings, of down, beyond comparison superior to what is called otter-down', and indeed such, that its 'many excellencies cannot be here set forth.'" Johnson, something tells me, did not swing that way.

Mattress historians note that right-thinking Brits and Americans clung to their feathers-on-the-bottom orientation until well into the late twentieth century. In the 1970s, duvets began to appear in department stores in England; in 1987 IKEA opened its first store in London, marketing duvets as "doonas." That was that. Today, according to the *Daily Telegraph*, department stores sell seven duvets for every blanket. The *Telegraph* reports, "Argos, the country's biggest furniture retailer, does not even sell woolen blankets. Fleecy little throws from man-made fibre, yes, but not a proper, woven piece of Britain. It stocks over 100 different duvets."

My wife took me to Macy's the other day, more for company than for my opinion. We went sheet and duvet shopping. This stuff will go on her parents' bed in Italy, a bed we now sleep on a couple months of the year.

This bed is an instrument of torture. Until recently its wool-stuffed mattresses rested on a bouncy, noisy wire mesh that over time had become fatigued and taken to sagging in the middle. The lumpy mattresses also sloped toward the center, creating a kind of culvert in the middle of the bed. These mattresses were heirlooms to her, pieces of family history she wanted to preserve. She said they just needed to be fluffed.

Fluffed? I pictured us hanging bedding out the window and pummeling our wool mattresses, punishing them for hurting us. Instead, we are now rehabilitating the bed. Persuaded by pain and bad sleep, she relented: The wool mattresses are history. The mesh is next.

But it looks like there will be a duvet.

While I wait beneath a Martha Stewart poster at Macy's, my wife tests sheets for crispness. She looks at Westport 1000 thread count, pronounces it slimy; Genova 1200 thread count, slippery. Next there's Bentley 400, Charter Club Opulence 800, and Ralph Lauren RL 624 Sateen, none of them quite right. She says she wants them scratchy. She skips the sheets and moves to duvets.

Martha Stewart looks down on me with that confident smile of hers. She's wearing pajamas. "It's already decided," she says. "You're getting a duvet."

"I know that."

"You know what else is nice," Martha says, "for accent?"

"I like the scratchy sheets. I'll give her that."

"Shams." She flashes me her Martha smile. "Lots of shams."

"No."

"King or queen?"

"Queen. No shams."

"In a variety of sizes," she says, "you can fit up to a dozen pillows on your bed."

My wife steps up to the register, motions me over. She's picked out a duvet cover. "The duvet," she says, "will be a special order. Is that okay?"

It's not. It's really, really not. But I tell her, "Of course, that will be fine."

31

The Quality of Your Sleep

I'm lying in bed reading a short novel by Gianrico Carofiglio on my Kindle. Guido Guerrieri, Carofiglio's funny, sad, world-weary lawyer from Bari, is standing in the doorway of a woman's apartment. He holds two bottles of wine and smells dinner within. Since his wife left him, he's been in a deep funk. His sleep is bad. He's given to spontaneous bouts of crying. In the interest of getting his life back together, he moves to a new complex and discovers one day this woman, Margherita, who lives two floors above him. Or rather, she discovers him, and invites him to dinner.

During this chat in the doorway, he makes a joke. "*Rise*," Guerrieri says. Meaning, in Italian: she laughed. *Rise. Sempre con quella specie di gorgoglio.*

My Italian is good enough to understand that Guerrieri hears something funny in her laugh. What I don't get is "gorgoglio." She laughed, once again with a kind of . . . what?

I touch the word "gorgoglio" on screen. Kindle highlights it and goes to its Italian dictionary, which I decide to bypass. Reading the definition of a word you don't know in a language that you only sort of know can be dicey. Plus, it's nighttime. I don't want to work.

I touch "More" in the dialogue box and ask to see the translation in English.

Hubble.

She laughed, once again with a kind of . . . hubble?

I'm not sure what laughter with hubble sounds like. I touch "gorgoglio" again and drag-select the whole sentence; then I click "More," "Translation."

She laughed, once again with a kind of gurgle.

Got it.

Guerrieri notes this detail and steps inside. Margherita shuts the door.

While I read, my wife stirs beside me. Her back to me, she is mostly asleep. I hold still, lying on my back, careful not to disturb her.

I've been reading on this Kindle in bed for some months now. It's backlit, which means I can read in the dark. There's a childish pleasure in that, a throwback to the flashlight under the covers. Except this is different. Two or three times a week I'm likely to wake from deep sleep at 2:00 or 3:00 a.m. In a moment, I'm fully awake. What do you do? Lie there and wait for your thoughts to dissipate and sleep to return? How long do you wait? Pre-Kindle, after twenty or thirty minutes, I would get out of bed and go downstairs, lie on the couch, and read. A couple of pages of *The Faerie Queen* can be as good as an Ambien. Now I stay in bed. The device weighs seven and a half ounces. If I want to, I can bring the complete works of Spenser and Plato and Shakespeare to bed, without worrying about crushing my chest.

There's lots of advice these days on how to sleep—how to go to sleep, how to stay asleep. Exercise. Seek bright light during the day and avoid bright light at night to calibrate your circadian rhythms. Don't take naps. Avoid spicy food and alcohol in the evening. Smart phone, computer, TV: shut them down an hour before you go to bed. Use your bed, the National Sleep Foundation advises, for sex and sleep only.

One day I ask my friend who is a sleep doc, should I be getting more sleep?

"I get, like, four to six hours," I tell him. "Seven if I'm lucky."

He turns his head, listening in his doctorly way, and says nothing, which I take as a request for more information.

"Maybe four to five hours uninterrupted. Once in a great while six."

"How do you feel?" he asks.

"Good," I say. My biorhythm bombs every day around four o'clock in the afternoon. I tell him that. "Shouldn't I get eight hours?"

"You feel okay," he says.

I nod.

"If you feel okay, I'd say you're probably okay."

Eight-hour sleep may in fact be a modern convention—and an error. Gregg Jacobs, a sleep disorder specialist at University of Massachusetts Medical School, observes, "For most of evolution we slept a certain way. Waking up during the night is part of normal human physiology." Historians point to hundreds of references to segmented sleep—first sleep, then second sleep—in medieval literature and medical texts. Back then, it was dark at night, very dark, all night. Nightlife, such as it was, could be dangerous. At sundown, people went to bed, slept soundly, and then woke for an hour or so, for reading, for prayer, for sex, after which they went back to sleep. Then came light and more light. In the 1650s Paris began to light the streets. In the 1690s London did so as well. Nightlife became a thing. Around this time, the word "insomnia" makes its first appearance in the English language.

Then there is electricity and a lot more light.

By the twentieth century, our thinking about sleep has made a dramatic shift. There is sleep resistance. To sleep begins to seem like a waste of time. (I remember saying, as a college student, probably right after reading Jack Kerouac, that I didn't want to sleep, I wanted to live, I wanted to burn bright, I would sleep when I was dead.) And now there is the new normal: sleep eight hours. In our time, segmented sleep is an aberration. Today, when we wake up in the middle of the night, something is wrong. Sleep needs fixing.

Can it be fixed?

Should it be?

I read a few more minutes. Guerrieri's dinner with Margherita is fraught, confessional. She opens his wine, pours him a glass. They eat. For a *digestivo* he drinks brown tequila. Then, smoking Guerrieri's cigarettes, one after another, which explains her gurgling laugh, Margherita tells him a long tale, of her drinking problem, of her troubled courtship and failed marriage, and now of a period of recovery. *Poi restammo li' a parlare, ancora, fino a notte.* "We hung in there. We talked and talked, into the night."

I close my Kindle, and its light goes out.

I am awake.

Sometimes in the dead of night, you lie awake and there is a riot of thought, a profusion of images, memories. It's your wild mind coming at you, a mixture of mystery and the mundane. Why am I alive? Will the lawnmower start? Am I a good husband? A good father? Did I forget to thaw the chicken? What is it to die?

Before their second sleep, people once lay awake thinking thoughts like these. It must be normal human psychology. I can't imagine them thinking, *Drat, I wish I could go to sleep.* They must have thought, How curious, and sad, and funny, and dreadful. How wonderful to be so wide awake.

32

My Father, Going Deaf

A few weeks ago my father woke up almost entirely deaf.

He already had a significant deficit. For years he has worn hearing aids. One for each ear, they are a microphone, amplifier, and loudspeaker all in one small plastic device the color of ear wax. He pokes at them with his index finger to dial the volume up and down. He changes their batteries with the same ethic of care that he rotates the tires on his car. More often than not, through most of a conversation, they feedback and squeal like a miniature PA system. A sound anyone in the room can hear. He does not.

This deafness, I suspect, is in his genes. His mother was similarly deaf. But while my father has always been open about hearing loss, my grandmother was more of a covert deaf person. When you spoke to her and she inevitably did not hear what you said, she would act like she had heard at least some of it.

"I'm leaving for school now, grandma."

"The what?" she would say.

"It's been warm for October, don't you think?"

"The what?"

Eventually she made peace with her condition. Summer evenings she sat on the end of the davenport, a headset clamped to her ears, listening to baseball games. If she detected a faint shimmering in her presence, what might be a person (she was also mostly blind), she made strangled pronouncements: "Jim Northrup hit a double!" She shouted to hear her voice over the headset: "Two out in the seventh!" During the day, she listened to the news and shared headlines. "Today is John D. Rockefeller's birthday!"

The morning my dad woke mostly deaf, he sent out an email distress signal. *I can't hear.* Later he called me on his cell phone. We tried to talk. "I can't hear anything, son," he said. I heard in his voice a tone I'd never heard before, a combination of perplexity, fear, and grief.

That day he drove himself to his ear doctor, reassuring me, and himself, that it was a matter of routine maintenance. "I get clogged up," he said. "I'll just have him rinse out some of the crud. He did it once before."

Late that afternoon he called again.

"It's not crud," he said.

"WHAT DID THE DOCTOR SAY?"

"I don't know what he said. I couldn't hear him. But he's going to operate on my ears in two weeks."

"WHAT FOR? TO DO WHAT?"

"Operate in the office."

"WHAT FOR?"

"I just can't hear you, son," he said. "I'm sorry."

A few days later, I drive the ninety minutes north to his house to pick him up. We're going to see the doctor, this time with a pair of functioning ears, to find out what's wrong and what the doctor proposes to do about it. In person, I discover, my father's hearing is even worse than it is on the phone. On the kitchen table are scraps of paper where Jackie, his helping lady, has written notes to him. *I thawed a meatloaf for you. The oven cleaning will be done by three o'clock. You may smell something.*

I write him a note too. *No procedure today. Conference with the doctor.*

"Let's take my car," he yells.

When I turn the key in the ignition, the radio comes on in a blast, at full volume. It's so loud I duck. He doesn't notice when I turn it off. He puts on his giant black old-guy wrap-around sunglasses and fastens his seatbelt. We make the silent ride across the river, through town, down the five-lane road, toward Saginaw. I tell him it's cold, just to make conversation.

"What?" he yells.

Four inches from his left ear, I holler my meteorological observation.

He nods. "Just past the Catholic church on State Street," he yells. "On the left."

Years ago my wife and I visited an ear, nose, and throat doctor for a thyroid condition she had. His diagnosis was that her thyroid was sick, that it would continue to be sick for three months, that she could take steroids or aspirin for pain (she chose aspirin), and that eventually, with no active doctoring on his part, her thyroid would start to feel better, which it did. Twice when we went for appointments, the same little girl was there to have her cleft palate worked on. And both times, from the interior of the office, came her blood-curdling screams, sounds so awful, so harrowing, I would have been grateful to be made temporarily deaf.

At the office on State Street I drop my father off at the front door and go park the car. He checks in and takes a seat. While we wait our turn to see the doctor, he offers a number of conversation starters.

"Alfreda called today," he yells. "She talked to Jackie."

Next to the door, a woman and her daughter chat quietly while they wait. The little girl looks pleased to have been taken out of school. Whatever's wrong with them, it's not their hearing. Sitting a few seats over from us is another father and son team.

"The physical therapist comes Friday," my father yells a few minutes later. "Boy, she gives me a workout."

The receptionist, hearing this, starts to giggle. I nod and smile at her, gesturing for him to keep his voice down just a little. He holds up a finger, indicating he understands, and then closes his eyes and puts his head back. It's March, and the office's Christmas decorations are still up. From the sound system in the ceiling comes Christian rock, barely audible. There's a lot of traffic noise as cars swish past the office. The traffic reminds me: he can't hear. I wonder if it's conventional to have music in an office for people with hearing problems.

On a clipboard I borrow from the receptionist, I write a few notes for him.

The doctor may want to put tubes in your ears.

"Floyd had tubes put in," he yells. There's no stopping him.

Did it help? I write.

"It's hard to get a straight answer from him," he yells in reply. He closes his eyes again, pondering Floyd's or his situation. Just then the other father and son are called for their appointment. The son stands and waits as his father, like mine, lifts his whole body out of the chair, pauses, straightens it out, and with the help of a cane pushes himself mostly upright and achieves equilibrium. He waits a second or two, making sure he's steady, and then takes a step.

Our turn comes. The doctor shakes my hand when he comes in the examining room. He has a thick, bristly mustache. He is burly and prematurely gray and diffident, almost ill at ease. He's assisted by a thin woman between fifty and seventy with lots of suntan makeup and hair that looks like a wig. Her gaze, which follows the doctor, is nothing if not adoring. Wearing a white shirt with a bad tie and baggy black stay-press pants, he seems like a hesitant Wilford Brimley. He looks in my father's ears, asks how he feels in a soft voice—he better than anyone knows shouting is futile—and explains what he thinks we should do. My father gives him a look that's more blank than encouraging.

"He doesn't read lips very well," the doctor says, turning to me.

"You have a mustache," I say. He smiles, taking it as a joke, which is not how I intended it.

The doctor shows me a graph that charts my father's hearing loss. "He's just lost more than half of what little he had left," the doctor says, "probably because of an infection." He wants to make a little incision in each ear drum, drain off the fluid, and put in some tubes. "'Time or tubes' is what we say." He lets that sink in.

"Will he get his hearing back?" I ask.

"Not all of it," he says. "Not what he'd lost before."

I point at the graph. "But this?"

He says he thinks the tubes should help. We shake on it, and his assistant schedules the procedure and goes over the details with me, while my father looks on. *I'll explain everything in an email*, I write on the clipboard.

In the car, on the way back to his house, he yells over at me, "Did you have to take a none-of-your-business day to come with me to the doctor?" I tell him it's okay. What are those days for, anyway? He shakes his head. It kills him just a little to accept so much help. "The doctor," he shouts, "is a portly chap." He smiles, holds out his hands to outline the doctor's girth. A few miles down the road he breaks the silence again. "Tomorrow, he says, "I'm going to work on my garden tractor, get it ready for summer."

Time or tubes. I'll explain that in an email or maybe on one of Jackie's scraps of paper.

"This car," he says, "has a nice, quiet ride." He looks across the dash, toward what happens next, toward home, obviously pleased with this little witticism. I think: *Tell me another one, dad. I'm all ears.*

33

No Secrets, Victoria

I was surprised recently to see this image appear every time I went to the Wix website: Heidi Klum, holding underpants. It's a delicate subject, underwear. Personally, I'd rather talk about something else.

Wix is a let-us-host-your-website site. You would think images would scroll, to advertise a technical feature of their web-composition kit. They don't. It's all Heidi, all the time, stretching those shorts. They look very stretchy. Which got me thinking about microfiber.

Some years ago I took a group on an excursion in Italy. We went to churches and museums in Florence and rode around Tuscany a little. It was a see, eat, shop, and relax trip. Among the travelers was one of my co-workers and his wife. He was a humanist who also happened to teach welding. One day over a dish of pasta he announced he had just bought some microfiber underwear. His wife Pam nodded. Both had an unmistakable twinkle in their eyes.

"What's that?" I asked. I thought of myself as a sophisticate at the time, but when it came to underwear, I knew I was hopelessly retrograde and low fashion.

"High-tech," Don said,

"Lightweight," Pam said.

"Durable," Don said.

Then they looked at each other. Again, the twinkle.

After lunch we went to the church of Santa Maria del Carmine. It's a church not everyone gets to, across the Arno, well worth the walk, famous for the Brancacci Chapel. Inside the church, begun in 1268, Don pointed at a column, shook his head, and commented. Artists and architects, he said, get all the credit. Think of the man who worked on that column, coming to the job every day, carrying his tools, hammering away at tiny details in just one part of the church. How many columns did he detail in his lifetime? Did he have days off? Did he bring his wife and kids to the worksite so they could appreciate the scope of the project and see his small contribution? Did he live to see the doors of the church open?

From there we went to the chapel, where we saw the Masaccio frescos, known in particular for an image of Adam and Eve being cast out of the Garden of Eden. On their faces they wear a devastating look of grief and shame. They know they are lost. They know they are naked. Thus begins, in human history, our life of toil, our knowledge of sin and death, and, as the other Masaccio frescos in the chapel show, humankind's need for the New Adam and the Church.

Thus too begins, it could be argued, the history of clothes. And underwear.

Underwear history is sketchy. The Egyptians wore loincloths, the Romans an undergarment called a *subligaculum*. In medieval times men wore "braies," from which we get the term "breeches." Braies looked a lot like shorts, with a drawstring at the waist, and were a garment that could be pulled down and drawn up, explaining the term "drawers." The history of women's underwear, a problematic subject given gender politics, is sparse. Did they or didn't they? The skirt and miniskirt had not been invented, making an answer to the call of nature, with long, voluminous dresses and shifts to manage, a complicated task. Pants were out of the question. (See Joan of

Arc.) It was thought, until a recent, exciting discovery, that perhaps women wore no underwear at all.

Then from Lengberg Castle, in Austria's East Tyrol, came a trove of textile finds the contents of which have significantly advanced our understanding of underwear history. The castle dates back to 1190; in a fifteenth-century castle-improvement project, a second story was added to the structure. In this second story, in 2008, a vault was uncovered, revealing medieval bras and underpants. Beatrix Nutz (that's her real name), an expert in medieval and textile archeology at University of Innsbruck, has studied this find and speaks to its advancement of brief history. She asserts, "Trousers and underpants were considered a symbol of male power and women wearing them were pugnacious wives trying to usurp the authority of their husbands, or women of low morality." For the historical record, Nutz notes that both Eleanor of Toledo and Maria de' Medici owned underwear, as did Elizabeth I. In a description of an effigy of the great queen of England, there is mention of a corset and drawers.

A day or so later, we were getting ready to board a bus, taking to the hills around Greve to taste some wine. Don had a puckish look on his face.

"Today," he said with a broad smile, "I'm walking with ease and comfort in my new microfiber underwear."

"Cool," Pam said.

"It's a weave that breathes," Don said.

Well, all right then, I thought.

I found some at the outdoor market in Piazza Santo Spirito. I made a couple of loops around the piazza, looking at cookery, dishware, linens, and food until I found socks and underwear. I pointed and said to the vendor, "Do you have microfiber? Medium, I think."

She laid out a few pairs of briefs on the table, all black, and then picked up another pair and gave them the Heidi Klum stretch. "Three for ten euros," she said.

I picked up a pair. They felt soft to the touch. Lightweight, as Pam said.

In white print across the front of the briefs was written, in English, in a font way too large, "SEX. KISS." I handed them back. "Is this all you have?"

The vendor nodded.

Could I do it? Could I buy underwear with those words emblazoned across my (lower) abdomen? What on earth were Italians thinking? What would my wife think?

The Italians I know over there, in fact, seem to have a special feeling about underwear. I've been to a number of birthday parties, dinners where gifts were presented to the happy lady, almost always including dainty, minimalist lingerie. And she raises them aloft for all to see; and we toast her and her underwear. No secrets, Victoria. It's simply a different attitude about *sex, kiss* than we have in the United States, especially the Midwest: playful vs. puritanical. On beaches in Italy men opt for briefs; American men are more likely to go with the baggy look, what Italians call, with a small hint of sarcasm, *braghe* (see "braie").

I bought them.

Don was right: comfortable, lightweight, technologically up to date. In further Italy excursions in the years after that, I used to joke with travelers who joined me that, in the interest of traveling light, I took only two pairs of underwear with me, the ones I was wearing and the additional pair in my suitcase. "Miracle fabric," I said. "Wash when you go to bed. They're dry in the morning."

So: I can wear SEX. KISS. (I might even be wearing them right now.) There remains this worry, a sorry cliché but a worry nonetheless: what if I'm in an accident? I'm sure healthcare professionals don't bat an eye as they scissor underwear off an injured person. It's not as if they look and make a note of what the patient was wearing. If they do, these days, the digital medical record might look like this: Underwear: ☺, ☹ (Please check one).

34

Flip-Flops and the
Leaning Tower of Pisa

The first time my wife took me to Italy after we were married, I wore
flip-flops. It would be stifling, August-hot over there. I planned on
wearing short-shorts and sleeveless T-shirts as much as possible,
to maximize exposure to sun and air. And flip-flops. These were
nice flip-flops I had bought at Pier 1, with rattan footbeds and royal
purple velvet thongs, anything but ordinary. But no sooner did we
arrive than she started to insult them.

"I can't believe you wear those things," she said.

I looked down, turned a foot, and admired the rattan. "Comfortable," I said. "Naturally cool."

A dismissive shake of the head.

I pointed to the purple thong. "And elegant."

"You don't see Italians wearing those things."

Those things. She couldn't bring herself even to say their name.
Flip, flop. Flip-flop. In truth, I did not see any Italians wearing flip-
flops. Neither did I see envious looks from passersby on the streets.

"Why don't you get some *ciabatte* like Domenico's?"

Domenico, her cousin, was an arbiter of fashion. In a state of relax,
he wore both plastic beach ciabatte and wooden clogs. That summer

it was obvious clogs were the most popular mode of transportation for Italians. On sidewalks you'd hear people clopping in and out of stores and trattorie, to and from the beach, like so many fashionably clothed horses. Clogs, I could see, were hot.

A few days later, at the *mercato* in Rimini, weary of hearing my footwear slandered, I picked up a pair of clogs, smooth blond wood with a wide blue leather band to fit over the bridge of the foot.

"Yes," she said.

No, I discovered repeatedly over the next week or so.

When we were kids, we called them thongs, not flip-flops. The first time I ever wore a pair was in the Straits of Mackinaw. The bridge was only a few years old, and my paternal grandmother wanted to see it in the worst way. "Daddy," she'd say to my grandfather, "wouldn't you like to see the bridge?"

He'd take his pipe out of his mouth, shake his head, and say, "No."

Her sight and hearing were fading. She must have felt a sense of urgency.

"Why not?" she'd say.

"I've seen a bridge," he'd answer.

Then one Thursday night late in the summer she called us and said Daddy was ready, and shouldn't we go before he changed his mind?

We left early the next morning, drove north, and camped that night in a park at the base of the bridge, not far from Fort Michilimackinac. While my grandparents sat in lawn chairs through the afternoon, regarding the bridge, the rest of us did what seemed like the only sensible thing. We went swimming in the Straits. The water was cold and rough. We expected that. And the bottom was rocky, so rocky as to be almost impossible to navigate. My parents must have figured swimming was going to be essential, maybe the only thing, outside of the fort, that my brother and I would enjoy, because they loaded us into the car, drove to a nearby five-and-dime store, and bought thongs for us. (This was before the advent of swim shoes.) They came in one color: blue.

In theory, it seemed like a solution. In practice, it was a disaster. Thongs, we discovered, were more floatation device than barrier between your foot and sharp rocks. Take a step and one fetched loose and bobbed to the surface. When you reached for it, your toes clenched to hold the other one on. The moment you relaxed the second one also slipped free from your foot. In an act of desperation we tried tying them on with nylon clothesline. (This was before the advent of duct tape.) It was no use.

For a while after that, I associated thongs with frustration and failure, until they became flip-flops and, in my mind at least, inseparable from summer ease and freedom.

I flip-flopped into the theater twice this summer and saw movies that took me back to early adolescence in all of its fullness—the ease and freedom, but also the confusion, self-doubt, and fear. In *Mud* I saw myself and a couple of friends at the county park in Lake City. We were lords of the lake. We patrolled the park on bikes. We sauntered on the beach in flip-flops. We had girlfriends. They looked at us, when they looked at all, in an irresistibly alluring way. *Chase us*, their looks said. *But don't catch us . . . because you are gross.* We were ten years old. We were gross.

One friend, Shawn Dryer, wore his hair in a crewcut. He was thin and sinewy, a natural leader, ready for anything. When we came upon a bubbling mud puddle in the pavilion parking lot one afternoon, it was Shawn who reached into the water and pulled out a chunk of dry ice. He tossed it from hand to hand, blowing on it. Then he took his investigation to the next logical step. He popped it in his mouth and swallowed it.

He smiled and tilted his head, thinking with his stomach.

"Well?" we said.

"It makes you burp," he said.

In *The Way, Way Back* I saw myself again, this time in the way back of one of those giant station wagons popular at the time, gazing out the rear window, no idea where we were going. I had something on my stomach my mother thought was ringworm. I'd walked around all that morning with my fly down. No one had told me until it was a joke. Now, worst of all, I was sickened by the unmistakable scent of dog poop. Sitting next to me was Don Booth, whose nickname was Foot (rhymed with "boot").

"Leaping lizards!" he said.

It smelled awful. And it was coming from my direction.

"Is that you?" he said. "Criminy, is that you?"

I looked at my foot. Fortunately I was wearing shoes that day, light canvas tennies with a curving blue line on each toe, an upside-down smile. There it was on the sole of one shoe, a smear of poop.

"Stop the car," Donnie yelled.

I was mortified, thinking, as any kid would, *Why does everything happen to me?*

Most mornings that summer we went to the park store for penny candy—straws full of colored sugar, miniature wax coke bottles with amber liquid sugar inside, ropes of red and black licorice. It was in that store, in August, we heard news that Marilyn Monroe was dead. It was a hot, sunny day. I didn't know much about death. I'd seen a few ancient relatives, stiff as manikins in their caskets, hands peacefully folded. I didn't know much about Marilyn Monroe either. She had not yet become an icon. If there were movies and photographs, other people saw them. To me she was mostly just a name. Found dead.

We walked down to the lake and looked across the water.

"She killed herself," Shawn said. "She took pills and killed herself."

How could she do that? I wondered.

"And did you hear?" he said. "She was nude."

This detail somehow made her death more terrifying. To be dead was unthinkable. To be dead and nude was even worse. We looked at each other and ate our candy. Nothing made sense. From a radio in the parking lot came the Beach Boys singing "Surfin' Safari." How many weeks of summer left? We tore off our shirts, kicked off our flip-flops, and crashed into the water.

Clogs and I were not made for each other. I kept falling off of them.

"I can't walk on these things," I said to my wife. We were in Nuovo Fiore, an ice cream shop in Riccione. "It's like they roll or something."

"You don't know how to walk," she said.

I had just picked myself up off the sidewalk outside. I was a danger to myself. Now I watched fashionable people clogging up and down the streets. What did they know that I didn't?

"You'll catch on," she said.

I kept trying. But I didn't.

The previous summer, another cousin, Vincenzo, had visited us in the United States. I had taken him fishing one day on the Saginaw Bay, where we caught half a dozen perch. It was more leisure fishing than sport fishing. He was determined to return the favor. He knew a little English; I knew a little Italian. With my wife's help, he explained he wanted to take me to the Leaning Tower of Pisa. My wife rolled her eyes. (No Italian I've met since was remotely interested in the Leaning Tower of Pisa.) I said sure, I'd go.

The next day he picked me up in a red Fiat convertible.

There are stretches of autostrada between Bologna and Florence that call to mind the Pennsylvania Turnpike, lots of hills, lots of curves. Only these were European drivers. Vincenzo drove like a madman, determined, I think, to wow me with his car. While he drove, we tried to talk.

He said, "I like a good Coca-Cola."

"What's the speed limit?"

He said, "My Aunt Tita is ninety years old."

"It would be all right to slow down."

He said, "Today we will ask for our spaghetti molto al dente."

"Are we almost there?"

He said, "Later I will take you to a town where only ugly people live."

At that time, it was still possible to climb to the top of the Leaning Tower. Vincenzo said he would pass on the climb. To me, it seemed like a good idea. From the ground I counted seven levels. A narrow spiral staircase corkscrewed around the perimeter inside the tower, all the way to the top. As you ascended, you leaned with the tower, into the interior wall, then against the outer wall. Back and forth, lean in, lean out. At each level, you could step outside onto a *loggia*. By the third level, I was feeling dizzy. I poked my head out in the direction of the loggia, then kept going. Lean in, lean out. By the fifth level, I was stricken with vertigo. And I was teetering on my clogs. I skipped the fifth and sixth loggias. Finally I gained the top level. Terrified I would fall, I pulled off my clogs and walked in bare feet to a bench and sat down. Vertigo, I now knew, made you sick to your stomach.

What hadn't occurred to me was the Leaning Tower of Pisa is a bell tower. As soon as I sat down the bells began to ring. Seven deafening bells. There were vertigo-free children everywhere, darting from the high side of the tower to the low side, and there were traumatized parents calling to them. "Maura," one father kept saying, "be careful. Please, Maura." *Good heavens*, I thought, *the little shit is wearing clogs.* I knew my Galileo. If Maura and I fell from the tower at the same time, we would hit the ground below at the same time. I also sensed, given my track record over the last week, I was fully capable of falling from the middle of the tower, whereas Maura was going to be just fine.

I'd had enough. I picked up my clogs and slowly took the stairway down in bare feet, hoping I would corkscrew myself back to equilibrium. Later that night, when Vincenzo deposited me safely at home, I flung the clogs in the back of a closet, retrieved my flip-flops, and never looked back.

Dana Stevens, writing for *Slate* this summer, lodges this complaint against flip-flops: "[Their] use seems to transport people across some sort of etiquette Rubicon where the distinction between public and private, inside and outside, shod and barefoot, breaks down entirely." Dana Stevens is right. And I think that's my wife's beef. Dude, get some decent shoes (a very Italian point of view). I get it, totally. And yet, to jailbreak your feet, to give them good, clean air to breathe, and to slow down to flip-flop pace, the *fwap fwap fwap* of your footfall saying take your time, that's living. That's summertime. How many weeks of summer left? How many summers? However many there are, I'll take mine in flip-flops.

35

Ravioli, *Richard III*, and a Dead Bird

The entry was not what I expected to find: "Last night I dreamed I killed someone." I was checking a journal I keep to see where we ate those ravioli one year, the ones with the poppy sauce.

A friend of mine wakes up every morning and writes down his dreams. An otherwise right-handed person, he writes about them with his left hand. He's that serious about his dreams. I'm that serious about ravioli.

The dinner came back to me. A Sunday, flower day in the little town, it was warm enough to eat outdoors. Outside the restaurant, along a line of tables and umbrellas, the street was closed to traffic. It was crowded with strolling couples and families out to enjoy flowers in the square, flowers spilling from balconies, flowers in clay pots on stoops and stairways.

We were finishing an appetizer when my wife said, "Oh no."

I thought something was wrong with the food.

She motioned to the table next to us. A woman was holding a bird, cradling it in her hands. It was a swallow, obviously in critical condition. I hunted chickadees with a Daisy BB gun when I was a kid. When the birds hit the ground, mortally wounded, they did that same yawning thing, as if gasping for air.

I refilled our wine glasses. "Don't look."

We both took a sip. We both looked.

Our waiter came and set down two dishes and a platter of ravioli in front of us. Over the next twenty minutes or so, the woman used one of the restaurant's linen napkins to keep the bird warm. She rocked it. She squeezed drops of water from the napkin in the direction of the bird's beak, which was no longer yawning. We ate our ravioli and drank our wine, casting mildly disapproving looks in her direction. She had to notice. When she held the bird close to her face and blew in the direction of its beak, I thought, *What's next, chest compressions?*

Pigeons, Woody Allen observes in *Stardust Memories*, are rats with wings.

And little birds? Ornate bats.

"Disgusting," my wife said.

The next morning, beneath the note I made on the ravioli, was that single sentence. *Last night I dreamed I killed someone.*

I auditioned to be a murderer when I was in college. That fall I had a course in literature of the English Renaissance. *The Faerie Queen* was on the syllabus along with a lot of poetry, including Shakespeare's sonnets. The previous semester I'd had one of the Shakespeare courses. Elizabethan English sort of felt like my language. One day the prof announced the theater department was putting on *Richard III*. Maybe some of us would like to read for a part, see Shakespeare produced as theater. I'd never been in a play, but I had a cool hat. I decided to give it a try.

Over in Quirk Hall, I went to the designated office to inquire. "Sign up on the board outside to schedule a reading," the girl said. She handed me four mimeographed pages, passages to choose from. There was some Richard, some Buckingham, some Hastings, and Catesby. I was no fool. I knew I didn't stand a chance getting a lead or main character of any stature. But maybe something small and pithy. I could be happy with a distant secondary role. I skimmed some lines spoken by an assassin. They looked like something I might want to say.

"Wish me luck," I said to the girl.

"Great hat," she said with a smile.

Yes, maybe I could do this.

Then again, maybe not.

The problem wasn't reading the words. It was saying them out loud and not sounding like a complete idiot. In act 4, scene 4, the assassin, named Tyrrel, says:

> The most arch deed of piteous massacre
> That ever yet this land was guilty of.
> Dighton and Forrest, whom I did suborn
> To do this ruthless piece of butchery,
> Although they were flesh'd villains, bloody dogs,
> Melting with tenderness and kind compassion
> Wept like two children in their deaths' sad stories.

There was more. The soliloquy was about the slaughter of children. For a few days I practiced reciting these lines, mostly in my car (I didn't want anyone to hear me), trying to find the proper tone of horror and remorse. "The tyrannous and bloody deed is done," I'd say and then look at myself in the rearview mirror. It didn't sound right. I didn't look like a killer. When I delivered this line, I might as well have been saying, "The mayonnaise and mustard sauce is gone."

The director was on loan from Reading University in England. He was tall and thin, with short dark hair and sideburns, and spoke, not surprisingly, with an English accent. He reminded me of the British character from *Hogan's Heroes*, only moodier, darker. For the audition, he and his wife and the assistant director sat at tables they had pushed together in the front of a classroom. There was a dish of chocolate chip cookies on the table. I said my name when

I came in, and the director found me on his list. While I read my lines, they looked on. The assistant helped himself to a cookie. How many times had they heard the assassin that day? If it was difficult for me, it must have been torture for them. Somehow, I got through it.

"Right," the director said. "It's a wonderful speech, isn't it?" His wife and the assistant both nodded. "Thanks very much then," he said. "Check the board on Monday."

It turned out I got two speaking parts. One of my characters had no name, the other a title, Page. Over the next couple of months, I learned that Shakespeare produced as theater meant a lot of waiting, coming to the theater four hours a night to say this line once: "Towards Chertsy, noble lord?" It was my first time hanging around theater people, who all seemed to have emigrated from a strange foreign country where everyone is in character all the time. Even when they weren't in their *Richard III* characters, they were in character. Sitting around waiting, I began to have doubts about myself. I was just sitting there. I wasn't, you know, *sitting there*, in a meaningful, intentional kind of way. What was my character?

For about two weeks, near the end of rehearsals, we worked on a carefully choreographed battle scene. We would fight to the death in slow motion, with a strobe light to enhance the effect. I'm pretty sure I got to kill someone. I'm also pretty sure I was one of the first ones to die, a directorial decision I completely respected.

My biggest moment came in act 4, scene 3, when Richard III motions for the Page (hey, that's me!) to approach him. He says:

Know'st thou not any whom corrupting gold
Would tempt unto a close exploit of death?

Down stage, right at the edge of the orchestra pit, Richard said these lines to me every night. And every night, when he did, he reached out, grabbed me by the throat, and scared the living crap out of me. He was a real actor (whom I have seen on TV for years since). If I didn't respond, he tightened his grip on my throat.

The casting, it turned out, was pure genius. Leave it to the British guy to know these things. I was supposed to stutter and croak in the presence of this malevolent force.

> I know a discontented gentleman.
> Gold were as good as twenty orators,
> And will, no doubt, tempt him to any thing.
> His name, my lord, is Tyrrel.

That said, I was dismissed to seek out the assassin, who would commit a tyrannous and bloody deed. And I waited, hiking up my tights, getting ready to kill and be killed.

When I ask my friend if he thinks dreams mean anything, he looks startled. Then lights go on inside him. It's precisely the way I would react if someone asked me how I feel about risotto with truffles. "Yes," he says, "dreams most definitely mean something."

We talk for a few minutes about my dream, or the trace of it left scrawled in my food journal. He's read Jung. We have all these potential selves inside us, Jung says. They speak to us in our dreams.

"So I could have a killer inside me?"

"Sure." He nods and begins to smile, pleased with the thought. "A little one," he says. "Why not?"

Killers inside us. I wonder what the woman dreamed that night, if she dreamed of giving life. Maybe she dreamed she revived the swallow, that it soared from her hands and became a brilliant flower in the cloudless sky above that town. Or maybe she dreamed it awakened, yawned, and flew into my face, clutching at my eyebrows with its claws.

Or maybe she dreamed that it swooped down on our table, snatching ravioli with poppy sauce from my plate, and flew away. That would have killed me.

36

Apri la Porta

It's a Tuesday night, and we're locked out of our apartment in San Marino. It could be worse. We speak the language. We're sitting in the bar up in the main piazza; for three euro I can buy a glass of red wine and eat all the free food I want. Except it's 10:00 p.m., and I've already eaten. I just want to go home and go to bed. Our rental car is parked down below the condominium. The car keys I have. So if worse comes to worst, we can drive up the hill and book into a hotel.

"Ask Aeneas for a locksmith's number," my wife says. Aeneas, our bartender friend, is pouring drinks for fifty or so people at the moment.

"What's the word for locksmith?"

"Just explain. The door is locked. The key is inside."

What's the worst? There's no local locksmith. Or there is a local locksmith, but he's on vacation in Yugoslavia. And when he finally gets back a couple of days from now, he can't just pick the lock; he has to drill it and replace it, which will take hours and cost us who knows what.

I've been waiting for this disaster to happen. Usually you know how to burgle your house. You know its soft spot, a window you left unlatched and can slide open, a back door with a lock you can jimmy. Or you keep a key outside somewhere. Our apartment has no back door. The side windows are two stories up, in back, three. I don't know where I would leave a key outside. There's so much *outside* outside.

"Don't you have someone you can ask for a key?" Aeneas shouts over the soccer game everyone is watching. "When this happens to me, I go upstairs and ask my parents."

I show him the set of keys my niece has brought us. Our key, I tell him, on our set, which I should be holding, is in the lock—inside the apartment, where I leave it so I don't forget it when I walk out the door. That's my system, obviously a failure.

Aeneas smiles, gives me a knowing look. "One of those," he says. The lock, he means. When there's a key inserted in the lock on the inside, a spare key inserted in the lock on the outside doesn't work. It just turns and turns in the lock, in neutral. It's a terrible feeling.

The number he gives us is 888-888. We get the cops on the phone. They give us another number: 888-866. The dispatcher says it may be awhile. There's another emergency at the moment. We take a seat in the bar. What's awhile in San Marino?

I've dealt with cops in Italy a few times. Years ago, I got pulled over. Wanded over, I should say. Here's how it works: A couple of cops in their baby blue Fiat stop by the side of the road. One of them, wearing his tall black boots, tailored pants, fitted waist jacket, and cap, holding an arrow-shaped wand, waves you to the side of the road. It's like an invitation. I don't know what they would do if you kept on going. Use the wand to commandeer your car, perhaps.

I pull over, come to a stop, and buzz down my window. "What did I do?" I ask.

"Documents," he says.

Cars go swishing past us. I fumble my wallet out of my pocket, realize with a sinking feeling I don't have my passport with me. That might be against the law. Double trouble.

"Con calma," he says. Keep cool.

I hand him my Michigan driver's license and the rental car forms. He regards them with a bland look on his face, glances at me, and then nods.

"Va bene," he says, and wands me toward the road.

"What did I do?"

"You go," he says, wanding me away a little more vigorously.

So I went.

Ten months ago I got a parking ticket in Pesaro, a town down the coast. It was a secret ticket. I drove somewhere I shouldn't have, parked in a restricted area. A stealth photo was taken of my rental car's license plate and then transmitted to the authorities. They processed it and let me know by mail I owed sixty-two euro for illegal parking. Only it wasn't that simple. First they contacted the rental car company, asked for my mailing address in the States, and waited a few months for it; once they got my address, they waited a few more months—why I don't know—and then forwarded a six-page document to me in a hand-addressed envelope. It came registered mail, which I had to drive to the post office to sign for. Inside was a bad copy of the photographed license plate, a map of the scene of the crime, a verbal description of the infraction, the pertinent legal language, and instructions on how to pay the fine, which, by the time I got the mail, had tripled.

Still in Detroit, I emailed the cops in Pesaro and asked in my pidgin written Italian for an audience, which was granted, in perfect English. I could see Major Achille Manna on October 19 at 9:30 a.m.

I arrived fifteen minutes early and presented myself to a Lieutenant Mariotti. I explained I was there to see Major Manna. The lieutenant wore stylish glasses (clear frames, red bands), a white shirt and tie, and a navy blue police blazer with stripes and gold braid. He looked dazzling. I had been mentally rehearsing my police station Italian. *I am guilty. I am responsible. I am sorry. Had I known, I would have paid on time.*

When I was shown in to see him, the major was sitting behind his desk. No blazer. He wore a white shirt and tie and reminded me a little of Dom DeLuise. He was ready for me. He lifted a four-inch stack of tickets and shook his head. The sight of them, I think, made him tired, made him hate his job and probably me.

"These are all rental cars," he said.

I am guilty.

"We have to contact all these companies—Maggiore, Autoeuropa, Europecar, Sixt, Car in Sicily, Hertz."

I am responsible.

"Do you know, Mr. Bailey, how much work it is to process all of these?" He dropped the mass on his desk.

I was holding my ticket and documents in my lap. He reached for them, pulled out the page with the bad photo, and showed me. Then he turned to the map and showed me the area, Castelfidardo. This, he said, was a clearly marked area, limited access, residents only.

I am sorry.

"Had I known, I would have paid," I said. "Ten months have passed, and the fine now is 180 euro."

He shook his head, laid a big hand on the stack of tickets.

"It seems excessive," I said.

"You think so."

The meeting was not going well. I thought about how many dishes of pasta, how many liters of wine I could buy with all those euro. Thursday was market day up the mountain in Borgo Maggiore. I wanted to buy a coat. One year, at the rental car stand in Bologna, the representative told me the police will eventually forget about tickets if you wait long enough. Six months, he said, and you were free.

"Always?" I asked.

Yes. Maybe. He shrugged. Who wants to test that theory, when the rental car company has your credit card number?

The major tapped my documents and chewed at his cheek. Now what? Why would they grant me this meeting if they were going to make me pay the full amount? We sat with our guilt and frustration a long moment. Then he flipped to the payment instructions in my documents and inked an *X* next to sixty-two euro.

"Pay the lieutenant," he said.

I thanked him and said, "I hope I don't see you again." He looked at me askance. Then he saw: I was making a joke.

"Not here, anyway," he said.

We've been waiting at the bar half an hour or so when a firetruck pulls into the piazza in San Marino. The door on the driver's side swings open and a tall fireman climbs out. He's wearing overalls and boots. I walk across the piazza to him, and he asks me if I'm Canducci.

"My wife is," I say.

He opens the back door and tells me to climb in.

I've never ridden in a rig like this, and this one is a beauty, although I see now it's less firetruck and more all-purpose emergency response vehicle, very red, even at night. I tell him our building is just down the street. We'll walk, he can follow.

The building is a six-story condo with a stairwell and elevator near the front of the building. The stairwell has an echo. Every *ciao*, *buongiorno*, *buona sera*, and *salve'*, every hinge squeak, key jingle, and door closing resounds from basement to top floor, amplified by the echo.

It turns out there are two firemen, one tall, one short, and they are both immaculate, Platonic images of the fireman. They have a kit that consists of thin strips of plastic, which they begin slipping into the seams between the door and its casing, above and below the latch. Then they start shaking the door, in and out, sliding their strips of plastic up and down. It's a terrible racket; the banging and sliding echo in the stairwell, deafening.

The short one looks at my wife. "It's how we do it," he says.

"Won't you break the door?"

"Never."

"The neighbors," she says. "They must wonder what in the world we're doing in there."

The big one is shaking and pounding the door.

The short one nods and smiles. "Your neighbors," he says with a mischievous look, "when they hear this sound, will probably all be jealous."

In five minutes, we're in. We thank the firemen profusely, and they drive off to the next emergency.

Later we're in bed, lights off. My wife says, "Did you see those guys? Not a hair out of place."

"GQ."

"I've never seen an ugly fireman over here," she says.

Lying awake, I rummage through memory for uniforms I've worn. Cap and gown, boy scout, marching band. The band uniform was particularly terrible—heavy, stiff, oversized. It was like wearing Styrofoam. I played the trumpet and was part of the oozing green protozoa on the football field forming the letter *F* from Freeland. Or was the *F* for Falcons?

One fall afternoon my sophomore year, I found myself in a car with Cordell Bloomer and Terry Savage, heading west on Titta-bawassee Road in Cordell's '57 Chevy. A little past Curve Road he slowed next to a landmark, a DO NOT PASS sign, that would help him find a pint of Corby's whiskey he had hidden in the ditch. That day was my first taste of whiskey; it was also the first and last night I played the cymbals in the band, banging away at them like a fool, which I most definitely was that night. I could have brought shame to myself, to my school. One slip and I could have disgraced the ugly uniform I was wearing.

"Buona notte," someone says. A door slams somewhere in the building, echoing in the stairway. Behind our building, a scooter accelerates up the hill. I ask myself, as most adults probably do lying in bed just before sleep: *How in the world did I get here?*

"You know I was in the marching band?" I say to my wife.

"Hmmm."

"The uniform," I start to say, but decide to let it go.

I'm pretty sure I could find that spot again on Tittabawassee Road. And there might be a photo of me in that ridiculous uniform somewhere, in the 1968 school yearbook maybe. I certainly hope so.

37

Buongiorno

Every morning I walk up to the bakery and back, a total distance of two city blocks. Serravalle is a small town. You say *buongiorno* to just about everyone you meet. It's a sign of civility. But not all buongiornos are alike.

Hum the first three notes of the musical scale, do re mi. Around here, to someone you don't know, or to someone you would prefer not to talk to, if you make eye contact, you say "buongiorno" in a barely audible voice, sounding the first and third notes in the scale, do mi mi. The second syllable is stressed, but only slightly: buon-GIOR-no. Do MI mi. And you keep walking. There are fresh pastries up the street, after all. There's cappuccino to drink and a newspaper to read. When you greet someone you recognize, on the other hand, the greeting changes: buon-giorn-no, mi do do. Equal stress on each syllable, which is another way of saying no stress. The falling intonation, for some reason, is a little more welcoming, allowing a brief opening for a quick exchange of pleasantries—Rain? Cold. *I bambini?*—but you can pass on that if you're in a hurry or if you're not in the mood.

This morning, when I stepped out of our building, an old gentleman was walking up the street. I must have looked familiar. He gave me the second buongiorno, which I was more than happy to return. I'll talk to anyone.

He stopped and squinted at me. "Do I know you?" he asked.

He might have been eighty, which meant he could have known my in-laws years back. I told him who I was. We talked for a minute, and sure enough, there was history. He did know them. He had lived in the United States when my in-laws were there. He worked on some of the same job sites as my father-in-law.

We shook hands. "Duilio," he said. I leaned in, and he said his name for me again, twice. Duilio. Do-EEE-lee-o.

All those syllables. It was going to be fun greeting him, "Buongiorno, Duilio," which would require a third, more musical buongiorno. Eventually we might progress to the familiar "ciao."

I presented myself, Rick, conscious, as always, of my conspicuously monosyllabic name, also offering "Riccardo," which I do not like much, vaguely hoping more syllables made my name—and me—easier to remember.

In five minutes, he told me a little of his story. With his wife and two daughters, he had lived in the United States for fifteen years. Then they came back to San Marino. A common story, I pointed out. To this he wagged an index finger. His wife was sick, he said. There was no treatment for her over there, so they came back. When I wondered, he shook his head. No, she was gone.

"I'm sorry," I said. "And your daughters?"

"My daughter," he said, gulping air. His eyes squeezed shut; I thought for a minute he would laugh. He pulled a handkerchief out of his back pocket. After they came back, the older daughter never adjusted to living over here. She tried. He said she knew four languages. In the end she couldn't find herself here and moved back to the United States. He dabbed at his eyes a couple of times and apologized for crying.

"She lives in Florida now," he said, adding, "It's terrible for a father."

"The other daughter?" I asked.

"Good," he said. He held up a thumb and forefinger. "Due figli."
She has two children.

We stood together on the sidewalk. We shook hands again. He apologized again for crying. "Duilio," I said, "I'll see you."

Later in the day, I will make the short walk up town three or four more times. I go to the grocery store, I go to the butcher shop, I go to the coffee bar that has a strong wireless signal. Evenings, for the benefit of night air (and to force myself to stay awake), I walk up to the edge of town and then back down to our apartment. It takes five or ten minutes, unless there is someone to talk to. The old town is little more than one narrow street. Mornings and afternoons it gets clogged with pedestrian traffic, with wide buses that rock like ships in a narrow canal, with throngs of kids rushing to and from school.

Here everyone walks. There is so much buongiorno.

Maybe that's why I'm so aware of older people here. Because everyone walks.

Those walks I take up town, I see a dozen older gentlemen like Duilio. Three stand on the corner, avid conversationalists, tapping each other's chests with the backs of their hands, explaining points with expressive fingers. Others are doing the old man walk: leaning slightly forward, hands joined behind their backs, taking slow, deliberate, contemplative steps.

Early Tuesday mornings I stand next to women my age and older, buying fruits and vegetables from the vendor in the piazza. I ask, "Does anyone make a sauce with *stridoli?*" Three old women tell me their recipe. "What do I do with *lischeri?*" A panel discussion ensues. "When do you add lemon juice? Do you add it at all?"

Back home, in suburban Detroit, I see old people at the senior center (they have their own dedicated place)—on exercise machines, drinking coffee in a round table group I rarely join. I see seniors in grocery store parking lots, at the hardware store. There is something poignant about some of these sightings. An older man piles canned goods and frozen dinners on the cashier's conveyer. I think he must be heating food for himself, eating alone. An older woman slowly backs her car out of a parking spot, straining to see, sawing the vehicle back and forth. She takes forever. I think, *Why is she still driving?* The thing is, living there, she has to drive.

Simone de Beauvoir, in *The Coming of Age*, observed, "We have always regarded [old age] as something alien, a foreign species." At home, old age is like that, mostly impersonal. I don't know that man in the grocery store. I've never seen him before. I don't know that old woman trying to unpark her car. I've never seen her before. At home, I'm astonished at how infrequently I see people I recognize in public places. For over thirty-five years I've lived in that community. I know the houses, roads, stores, buildings. Every day back home, as often as I walk here, I'm in my car. I merge with traffic coming and going. I know the community the way I know my own home. Yet when I park in the lot in front of Trader Joe's and get out of the car, I often wonder, *Who are all these people?*

Maybe it's not the difference between Italy and the United States. Maybe it's the difference between a small town and suburb. Would suburban Milano feel like suburban Detroit? Doesn't Serravalle feel like Freeland?

"Buongiorno, Maria."

I'm walking home from the bar one morning. She's leaning against the wall outside the middle school, resting. The mother of one of my wife's childhood friends, Maria is ninety and is dressed in a black skirt and fitted waist-length jacket, her thick gray hair pinned back, a colorful scarf tied around her neck. She's going up to the bar for coffee, or she's going up to the church for mass. When I explain to her who I am, which I do every time I see her, she warbles something in dialect that I don't understand and then says, "I'm still here. Do you believe it?" She raises a hand to one of my cheeks, pulls me to her, and kisses the other cheek. She laughs her high, liquid, musical laugh.

There are two beauty shops in this town. My wife's aunt, also ninety, gets her hair done once a week. She describes the gaggle of widows that congregates there every Thursday. They discuss how wonderful it is being widows, with no husband to wait on or walk around or drag after them. It's so liberating once they're finally gone. One of the women says, "I keep waiting for my husband to die. I wait and I wait and I wait. He just won't die!"

And they all laugh.

Over the last day or so, I've re-read Philip Roth's *Everyman*, a book I brought over here with me five or six years ago. It's a dark novel, an unflinching meditation on old age, in tone somewhere between somber and harrowing. Near the end of the story, the main character finds himself living alone on the Jersey shore. Largely because of betrayals and mistakes he has made in life, now in his seventies, he is totally isolated, preoccupied with his accelerating physical decline. He gets news one day of three contemporaries, one dead, one dying, one diagnosed. "Old age isn't a battle," he says. "It's a massacre."

It must be a massacre here too. In the piazza, at the edge of school, and along the streets are small billboards with *manifesti* posted. These are reminders of those who have died, broadsheet posters with names, dates, and a line or two of text, many with color photographs of the departed.

I stop in front of a billboard one morning, across the street from the house where my wife was born. Enzo, the retired baker, is standing there too, looking.

"Buongiorno."

"Buongiorno."

On the board are four men my age and older (I picture their wives rejoicing) and a young man, twenty-one years old. I ask Enzo if he knew them.

"Yes, a couple of them very well. But sometimes, you know, the manifesti are from towns up the road"—he points up the mountain—"for the relatives and friends who live here. Everyone knows everyone." Pointing at the twenty-one-year-old, he says, "The young people, those are the hard ones."

A few months ago, a manifesto for my wife's uncle was posted there. When I was here two years ago, there was one for Enzo's brother.

"We're still here," I say.

"Yes, we are." He turns to me and smiles. "We're carrying the flag."

I rattle the package I'm holding, tell him I should get going. He knows what it is. Until he retired ten years ago, it was his bakery. The cake I'm bringing home this morning he must have made for years and years, hundreds of them, probably thousands. It's an inch thick, round, smaller than a pizza. The baked dough is dark brown, heavy with cooked grape must and raisins, topped with walnuts and almonds, and then drizzled with honey.

"Piada dei morti?"

"Yes," I say. Bread of the dead. They only make it in the fall, for the day and month of the dead. "My wife loves it."

"Bones?"

Yes, the baker tossed in a couple of cookies too, called bones of the dead. I rattle the package again. I'm ready to walk. "See you around, Enzo."

"Buona giornata," he says.

38

What's New

And then there is the hairdo. At some point during our time in Italy, we drive thirty minutes down the coast to Pesaro, where my wife goes to Marcello for shampoo, color, and cut. (I think that is the order of operations.) Unlike Serravalle, with its plodding small-town civility, and unlike Rimini, with its grubby charm, Roman footprints, and jarring internationalism (hello, Russians), Pesaro is fashionable, homogeneous, and a little bit smug. At Marcello they don't make appointments. My wife walks in. They take her coat. She gives herself to two hours of luxury.

This time it's a late weekday afternoon. After dropping her off, I walk in the direction of the Via del Corso.

Probably every old city in Italy has a Via del Corso. Without Google-translating it, I'd just call it Main Street, a principal artery through the city center, often with limited or no auto traffic. In Pesaro the Corso is a fashion runway. An occasional van crawls up or down the gently sloping brick street, making deliveries. Patient residents inch toward home in their cars. Mostly, though, it is well-dressed people on foot or on bikes.

I stop at a place called Bar Iris, hoping to find a Wi-Fi connection. I have the first chapter of Louis Begley's *Shipwreck* on my Kindle.

If it's engaging, and if there's Internet, I'll download the rest of the novel for later. Served an espresso and a shot of water (water first—order of operations), I ask about a connection.

"No Wi-Fi," the young woman says. Her hair is tied back in a bun. She has a tattoo necklace.

"Anywhere around here?" I ask.

"All blocked." She mimes turning a key in lock. "You need the password."

In that case, I tell her, I will have a glass of wine and then, considering it will be a long hair appointment, probably another glass of wine. I position myself so I can read and watch people walk by the bar. In short order I make a startling discovery.

Sweatpants.

Not just an occasional man who has drifted into sartorial error and foolishly ventured into public. No, I witness blue and gray sweatpants on many men, young and old.

This is odd for two reasons. I think it's safe to say the United States invented sweatpants. Usually a fashion trend moves from Italy to the U.S., not the other way around. Years ago my wife and I ran into a young woman at the airport in Rome. She was flying to the United States. She was someone connected to someone we knew in Pesaro, exceedingly well turned out, and wearing one of women's fashion's greatest gaffes: stirrup pants. It was summer. The pants were snow white. She looked like a model of a vintage skier prepared for photo ops on the slopes. It took a year or so, but eventually stirrup pants caught on in the U.S., where they lasted a long, long time. The other reason, of course, is the astonishing sight of a Pesarese dressed down, way down. I would have expected sweatpants in Pesaro to be like pornography in Kabul: indicative of a fatal cultural breakdown, a character flaw someone could indulge only at home, doors locked, shades pulled.

For years, arriving in Pesaro, the first stop my wife and I would make was Amadeus, a boutique run by her cousin Nano and his wife

Marisa. We stood on the floor just inside the door and exchanged kisses and news. Eventually Nano, conscious that we were smack in front of the big display windows, would move us away from the front of the store. "Go over there," he'd say with an impish smile. "If paying customers see you two in here, you'll drive away business." Then they would fix us up with some new clothes, my wife a lot, me just a little. One year Marisa slipped a double-breasted linen blazer on me. It was the color of sand, *sabbia* in Italian. "Nice," she said, tugging and straightening the jacket on me. "See how good you look? On you the sabbia is very beautiful." In truth, it felt a little crooked. I bought it anyway, feeling like I ought to make an effort. I took it home and waited five years to wear it. (Buy it, wait a while, and then wear it—order of operations.) She was right. It was beautiful. Maybe it's a Methodist fear of fashion. I just can't dress like an Italian.

Except for the scarf. I'm not afraid to scarf up.

My second glass of wine arrives just as a couple enters the bar, pulling their dog behind them. They sit at the table next to mine. It's warm in the bar, but they don't bother pulling off their scarves. I turn back to my Kindle. The narrator in this Begley novel, an American named North, is seated in a bar called L'Entre Deux Mondes. His story begins in Paris, circa 2003. When a waitress approaches him, Begley's narrator muses, "I have to admit that altogether I like the new kind of French. I like their healthy looks. So different from the sallow kids I knew when I was a kid myself, with their passion for politics and their yellow teeth that melted in plain sight as they drank their scotch."

Outside, a parade of pedestrians passes, many walking with arms linked, most wearing scarves. It's a week since the terrorist attack in Paris. I wonder about the new French that Begley mentions. I think of my Arab students back home in Dearborn, standing by the door outside my classroom, laughing, hugging each other, being innocent girls. Conscious of their politically charged appearance—

how can they not be?—they call themselves "scarfies" in perfect English and laugh the stigma away. They laugh; still, there is an undercurrent of fear. After 9/11 I worried about them, feared for their safety, knowing that, seeing their scarves and long dresses, an angry American might lash out: take revenge first, ask questions later. Order of operations.

The couple sitting next to me drinks tea. Their pooch, a dead ringer for the old RCA dog, seems happy to have a seat. I listen for conversation, straining to hear the dog's name. My niece tells me her friends like to give their dogs English names: Scott, Lizzie, Susie, Brad. This one is Spillo (SPEE-lo), which is the Italian word for a small, pointy object; the English translation is "pin." Walking past their table with a tray under her arm, the woman with the tattoo necklace leans down and tells the dog how good, how well behaved, how handsome he is, to which the dog responds with one crisp, preemptory bark.

They get up to leave around the time my phone rings. My wife is ready. I'm supposed to meet her at Amadeus.

"Let's go, Spillo," the man says. "Come on!" He pulls on the leash, but the dog won't budge. "Su! Andiamo." He pulls at the dog again, charmed by its intransigence. It's no go. I wrap my scarf around my neck and watch as he bends down and picks up the dog. Tucked under his arm, it asserts itself with one more piercing, sovereign bark.

Outside I merge with traffic. It's getting cold. I'm glad to have the scarf.

39

Small Beans

It's the little things that divide us.

My wife and I disagree on toilet paper orientation, whether the lap falls next to the wall (her way) or away from the wall (my way). When I take bread out of the fridge and give the wire tie a counterclockwise twist to open the bag, if the tie tightens, I know who closed it last. I feel a wave of dissonance, a visceral feeling of imbalance. It's like stepping onto an escalator that's not moving.

We disagree on how to load flatware into the dishwasher. My system is rational—forks on the left, knives on the right, spoons in the front and rear of the basket. Loaded like this, it's a delight to empty a dishwasher. She doesn't see it this way. "The spoons and forks nest," she says, giving me a look of gentle disapproval. "They don't get clean." She arranges flatware in a messy jumble. The way she loads, it takes twice as long to empty the basket. I won't have anything to do with it.

Then there are beans. We've had bean problems for years.

Her beans, I admit, are good.

We're in the hills above the Adriatic, a few miles inland, and just now dusk is bluing the meadows and vineyards that slope down to town. It's summertime, so all the windows in the trattoria are open. Like most Italian hill towns, this one has a fortress. The structure dates roughly to the year 1000; it was rebuilt in 1300. There's also a church and a few narrow picturesque streets and some shaggy trees in full leaf, all part of the breathtaking normal of this region. We're here, sixteen of us at the table, for the tagliatelle and beans.

These tagliatelle, what we would call fettuccine in the United States, are homemade, the pasta cut (*tagliata*) into ribbons, served with beans ladled over them. Maria, the proprietor, says it's quite simple: beans; carrots, celery, and onion; slices of *cotechino*, which is a sausage of pork and lard wrapped in pig skin; olive oil and *conserva* (tomato paste); salt and pepper and water. In three hours you get a soup cooked far enough beyond soup to make a beany, velvety brown sauce.

When the server lays four steaming platters on our table, all conversations stop. A breeze billows through white curtains. We regard these dishes with a combination of adoration and lust. Then someone says, "Chi vuole?" Who wants some?

Who knew beans could be so good?

Next day my wife says to her mother, "Guess what we had last night." Without waiting for her mother to answer, she launches into a description.

Mother waves a dismissive hand. "I know," she says. "We had that all the time when I was a kid."

"You did? But why didn't we?"

"Because it's peasant food," she says. "It's what we ate because we didn't have much money."

That's beans for you.

When I was growing up, a couple of times a month we sat down to a dinner of beans: a pot of navy beans boiled long and low, seasoned with salt and pepper, cooked far enough beyond soup to make a thick, savory, beanful broth. My father, a child of the Great Depression, called this dish "soupy beans." The navies grew at the edge of the farm town where he was raised and, thirty years later, at the edge of a different farm town where I was raised. They grew in forty- to eighty-acre fields—long, luxurious seas of green next to sections of corn and beets and soybeans.

We ate soupy beans ladled over bread. It's what they ate back then, he explained, because they didn't have much money. Beans were necessary. And delicious.

Our Michigan navy beans are delicious.

Trouble surfaced when I came home from Italy one year with beans on my mind. Tuscans are called *mangia fagioli*, bean eaters. Wherever you go in Florence, you find *fagioli all'uccelletto*, beans cooked in the style of small game birds. This means garlic, sage, olive oil, and tomato. For all of a month after that trip, two or three days a week I cooked beans all'uccelletto. It was a fine madness.

"Enough with the beans," my daughter finally said.

My son agreed.

"They're good," my wife said, "but not with those navy beans."

Those navy beans?

"But I love my navy beans," I said.

She shook her head. "Cannellini would be better."

Perhaps the recipe called for cannellini. But to insist seemed pedantic. And cannellini, I thought, when you bought them, who knew where they came from, how long they'd been sitting on store shelves? Whereas my beans came from my hometown. They were fresh. They could probably be dated to the exact time of their consignment, maybe even traced to a specific farmer and field (Vern Stephen, the corner of Hotchkiss and Garfield Roads). It was then I began to notice my wife's resistance to my beans. While I looked lovingly upon their blond goodness, she ate and shrugged them okay.

Just okay.

Beans are not a neutral food.

Thoreau was a bean farmer. "I came to love my rows, my beans," he writes in Walden. "They attached me to the earth." He rhapsodizes about beans, about farming:

> This was my curious labor all summer—to make this portion of the earth's surface which had yielded only cinquefoil, blackberries, johnswort, and the like, before, sweet wild fruits and pleasant flowers, produce instead this pulse. What shall I learn of beans or beans of me? I cherish them, I hoe them, early and late I have an eye to them; and this is my day's work. It is a fine broad leaf to look on.

Having grown up around bean fields and admired the plants' broad leaves, having driven country roads outside of town on warm July evenings and gazed down long rows of bean plants vibrating with color and vitality, I understand Thoreau's rhapsody. He was determined to know beans.

But Thoreau, that dope, did not eat them. So how could he truly know them?

He describes himself as a Pythagorean. These days, if we know Pythagoras, we know him for his theorem, $a^2 + b^2 = c^2$. Tenth grade geometry, right triangles, let c = the hypotenuse. But Pythagoras is also known for this famous maxim: don't eat beans.

The record, it should be noted, is not crystal clear. The *Stanford Encyclopedia of Philosophy* quotes Aristoxenus—a student of Aristotle, who was himself a great admirer of Pythagoras—claiming in 300 BC, "[Pythagoras] valued it most of all vegetables, since it was digestible and laxative." On the other hand, it appears Pythagoras bought into all manner of superstition associated with beans. Don't eat beans— they look like genitals. Don't eat beans—they resemble the doors of Hades; their stems connect this world to the underworld. Souls, which are essentially wind in that worldview, could be reincarnated through the bean plant, and thus to walk upon beans was to trample souls. It gets weirder. A chewed bean spat on the ground and warmed by the sun was believed to smell like semen or spilled blood. Weirder still was the belief that a bean blossom placed in a container and then buried would grow into a human head, and thus to eat beans was tantamount to eating your parents' heads and therefore a form of cannibalism.

Beans and the dead: it's a connection that survives to this day. On All Souls' Day, Italians remember the dead solemnly, if gluttonously, by eating almond cookies called *fave dei morti*, beans of the dead, or sometimes, because of their shape, *ossi dei morti*, bones of the dead.

In fact, it was the fava bean that bugged Pythagoras. The blossom has a black spot on it, and this perceived defect was enough provocation for Pythagoras to change the menu. Not me. I'll strip fava beans out of their pods, blanch them, tear off their jackets, and eat them raw, avid for their rich green color, their firm sweetness. It's a lot of work for a handful of beans, but when they're tossed with extra virgin olive oil and served with shaved Parmigiano or pecorino, it's a job I'll sign up for.

Saturday mornings at the local market north of Detroit, we buy Swiss chard and eggplant from Korean farmers. For a few weeks in midsummer they have cranberry beans, what the Italians call *borlotti*, still in their pods.

"These are good," my wife says. "You might try these all'uccelletto." I hear her underline *these*.

But I've come to my senses. Every bean has its place. And she's come to her senses, developing a newfound appreciation of the navy bean. On such mornings, fresh from the market, we sit at the kitchen table and shuck beans. It's slow going. It's bean work. It's a job our parents would have done hundreds of times.

I lift a handful of borlotti. They are creamy white with red speckles. After a few hours in the pan they are brown, bigger than navy beans, undeniably delicious.

"Why not," I say. I can swallow my reservations. They go down easy as beans. "Let's try them."

40

American English, Italian Chocolate

One September day in 1975 I was sitting in a classroom in North Carolina when a woman behind me tapped me on the shoulder. I was new to the school. I'd talked to a few classmates, but not enough, I thought, for anyone to know me. It was my first experience in the South.

"Wisconsin?" she said.

"What?"

She smiled and said, "You talk funny."

I told her she was close. How did she know?

It was the midwestern nasal, she said. It gave me away.

This was a course in American literature. In the weeks ahead I remember a classmate from Mississippi talking about the poet Hart Crane. "He was fixin' to write a modernist epic," she said. In another class, a student from Worchester, Massachusetts, said he looked forward to re-reading "The Hot of Dockness."

"Or as you would say," he paused and twisted his mouth sideways, forcing himself to make the *r* sounds, "The HeART of DARKness."

On December 21, 2013, the *New York Times* published a piece called "How Y'all, Youse and You Guys Talk." By the time I got to Facebook around 7:00 a.m. that day, there were already multiple links to the article (technically not an article but something called a "news interactive"). It must have lit up the Twittersphere. In the eleven remaining days of the year, "How Ya'll" generated more hits on the *Times* website than any other article (or news interactive) in 2013.

When I went to the *Times* site and checked out "How Y'all," I found a twenty-five-question quiz based on a Harvard dialect survey developed in 2002. Did I say "you guys" or "youse" or "yins"? Did I say "cougar," "puma," or "mountain screamer"? "Kitty corner" or "kitty wampus"? "Lightning bug" or "peenie wallie"? How did I pronounce the word "aunt"?

According to the survey, I was from Grand Rapids or Detroit. Or somewhere thereabouts. That's me. I'm nasal, and I'm proud. We love our local lingo.

One of my favorite skits on *Saturday Night Live* in the past few years is "The Californians," a goofy takeoff of daytime soap opera that lampoons Cal-speak. It features a bunch of suntanned So-Cal nitwits who delight in gossiping and giving each other driving directions. Best of all is Fred Armisen's California accent when he greets his nemesis. "Stuart?" he says. "What are you doing here?" But it sounds like, "Whhrryouooingere?" Consonants completely slid over, vowels stretching and gliding into each other. He doesn't speak the sentence. His mouth extrudes it.

Which brings me to chocolate.

I noticed in a recent headline that Hershey's is coming out with chocolate spread, not one but three different kinds. One is hazelnut chocolate spread, which, depending on your point of view, is either an homage to Nutella or a rip-off. The news release, published in the *LA Times*, reports, "[Hershey's] suggests putting the spreads on anything from graham crackers, strawberries and bananas, to celery, pineapple and pickles." Good grief. Can Hershey's take something indescribably wonderful and not ruin it? Pickles? Really?

The year we skied the Italian Alps, we stayed in a hotel next to the fire station in Courmayeur. This was Nutella country, my wife informed me. All of Italy, it could be said, is Nutella country. But all things are regional in Italy. The Piedmont is Nutella country because it is hazelnut country. Sometime in the 1940s, Alba pastry maker Pietro Ferrero combined hazelnuts and chocolate to make *pasta Gianduja*, which ultimately became what we know as Nutella today. I hope there is a statue in his honor in the city square.

Evenings after skiing all day, we walked past the fire station on our way up into town. We would hear commotion inside as four or five firemen, all cooking dinner, all standing in front of a stove with all the burners in use (and probably the ovens), yelled at each other in their dialect, a sort of preprandial foreplay. Once up in town, two or three consecutive nights, we found our way back to a narrow street of shops, where, halfway from the end, there was an open window. From the sidewalk you looked down into a small, warm kitchen. It was a crepe shop. On a board hung next to the window our choices were written, among them Nutella with mascarpone, Nutella with banana, Nutella with Grand Marnier, Nutella with *confettura di arance amare* and Grand Marnier, or if you really needed a fix, Nutella with Nutella. A late middle-aged gentleman wearing a white T-shirt and white apron cooked crepes for us while we waited in the cold.

Then we stood at the window, eating them. What if we wanted more?

Between bites we wondered out loud how anything could possibly taste so good.

He nodded. "It's what we do."

"I just hope you keep doing it," my wife said.

"Well," he replied with a tired smile, "who's going to do this when I'm no longer here?" He said his kids didn't want to make crepes. It was hard to find a young person who would learn the work, then stay with it the way he had. "The little place like this," he said, "all across Italy is disappearing. We have the supermarket now."

I thought of that window and the crepe man's lament some years later while I was attending a conference in Myrtle Beach. You go to a conference expecting bland, from the hotel room to the morning Danish and anti-coffee to the chicken luncheon. The whole experience has as much gustatory appeal as a grocery store tomato: the color is right, it stays fresh forever, but it's pretty much devoid of flavor. At least, I thought, we'd find some good local food out there.

Out there, in town, driving past alligator adventure and putt-putt golf courses and a gazillion T-shirt shops, past beachwear, golfwear, birdwear, and fishwear shops, past Christmas Mouse (open year round!) and Adventure Beach Paintball Park, I realized they had everything, from Fuddruckers to Wendy's to Godfather Pizza, which felt like another way of saying they had nothing.

"But what if we want to eat local food?" I was stopped at a gas station.

Behind her protective sheet of bulletproof glass, the clerk puffed on a filter cigarette and blew smoke back over her shoulder. "Local," she said, and asked if I meant, like, Ruby Tuesday?

"But what if we want to eat local food?" I asked at a few more stops.

Finally, an answer. "You can do that," a thin gentleman at a liquor store said. "But not here." His thick steel-gray hair reminded me of the hood of a car. He led me out the door and pointed south, said to drive down the coast to Murrells Inlet along the Salt Marsh Nature Preserve. "You'll find some shacks down there. Y'all like shrimp and grits?"

I said yes.

The truth is, he had me at "preserve." And "y'all."

In her 1984 novel *Dreams of Sleep*, Josephine Humphreys presents a South in transition. Her narrator ruefully observes, "The new South is Ohio warmed over." The subdivisions, the chain restaurants, the grocery store with "its long glassy facade papered with ads for Tide, Crisco, and canned corn beef." This is civilization, the narrator says, "proof of human omnipotence."

New South? With apologies to my friends from Akron, I would argue that much of the United States looks like Ohio warmed over. Pull off the freeway (or highway, expressway, thruway, interstate, whatever you call it) in Omaha, Stockton, Portland, Lexington, or Kalamazoo, and you'll see the same thing. When you pass the Bed Bath and Beyond, you'll know that Chili's is not far away.

It's all about the mouth: how we speak and, to a lesser extent, what we eat puts us on the map. I think that explains the popularity of "How Y'all." We don't want to be from just anywhere. We want to be from somewhere. After I completed the dialect survey and a map appeared on my computer screen with two points in a place I knew as home, I felt a foolish rush of pleasure. The survey knew me.

Which brings me back to chocolate.

February 5 is World Nutella Day.

That seems like a pretty good idea. But is it?

My wife thinks the Nutella we buy in the United States is not as good as the stuff in Italy. She points to the plastic jar and says that means something. Plus, she's been buying "designer" Nutella-like spreads over there for a few years now. She knows her stuff. Her discerning palate also tells her that since Nestlé bought Perugina chocolate (in 1984), the Baci (milk chocolate and hazelnut kisses) we buy in the U.S. are inferior to those they sell in Italy. And once again, I trust her instincts. In matters such as these I would trust her with my life.

Perhaps decline is general, all around the world.

If so, we should resist.

I should forego Nutella on February 5 as a matter of principle. I should just say no to the multi-nationalization of food. I have my principles. I should do that. But chief among my principles is the pleasure principle. So no, I will not stay the spoon. I'll celebrate Nutella day here the way it is celebrated in Ohio, which is to say all across the United States: tasting it, loving it, transported by it, half-wondering where I am.

SOURCE ACKNOWLEDGMENTS

"Big White Birds" originally appeared as "Duck Love" in *Skive Magazine* in September 2012.

"Sick Wild" originally appeared as "On Frogs and the Sixth Extinction" in *Storyacious* on July 23, 2014.

"The Man from Glad, Car Crash, Amnesia" is forthcoming in *Mulberry Fork Review* as "Glad."

"Clinical" originally appeared in *The Journal of Microliterature* on September 29, 2013.

"Love at First Shite" originally appeared as "Won't You Sit Down" in *Defenestration* on March 6, 2013.

"Feet First" originally appeared in *The Yale Journal for Humanities and Medicine* on November 15, 2011.

"For Donna, Ibsen, Pepys, Levitation" originally appeared as "Ghost Stories" in *Biostories* on December 4, 2013.

"The Soft Imperative" originally appeared in *Thread*, Fall 2016.

"Old Houses, New Residents" originally appeared in *Ragazine cc.* in the 2013 March–April issue.

"Chemical Neutral" originally appeared in *WritingRaw* in December 2011.

"Pure Corn" originally appeared as "Correct Cake" in *The Writer's Workshop Review* on September 30, 2012.

"Fly" originally appeared in *Fear of Monkeys* in December 2012.

"Bridge Failure, Heart Attack, Fava Beans" originally appeared as "Infra-structure" in *Drunk Monkeys* on December 5, 2014.

"My Father, Going Deaf" originally appeared as "All Ears" in *Cleaver Magazine* in March 2014.

"Flip-Flops and the Leaning Tower of Pisa" originally appeared in *Blue Bear Review*.

"Ravioli, *Richard III*, and a Dead Bird" originally appeared as "Page" in *Gravel* in March 2014.

"Small Beans" originally appeared as "Beans Squared" in *Emptysink Publishing* in December 2014.

"American English, Italian Chocolate" originally appeared as "Mouthy" in *Terrain* in March 2014.

CPSIA information can be obtained
at www.ICGtesting.com
Printed in the USA
LVOW08s1735180517
535029LV00002B/205/P

"In Rick Bailey's memoir, ̶ ̶ ̶ ̶ ̶ ̶ ̶ ̶ ̶ short essays filled with poetic language and the feel of a satisfying short story. In writing that is filled with quick humor and poignant tenderness, Bailey's experiences reflect our own humanity back to us."—M. L. LIEBLER, poet, editor, and author of *I Want To Be Once*

"Rick Bailey's writing sparkles with wit and self-deprecating humor, provoking laughter that hurts with the recognition of our own foibles and faults. His keen observations transcend the 'small' subjects of these short, powerful essays." —JIM DANIELS, author of *Rowing Inland* and *Eight Mile High*

"Rick Bailey is insatiably honest, addictively affable, meticulously observant, and beautifully precise."—LISA CATHERINE HARPER, author of *The Cassoulet Saved Our Marriage*

American English, Italian Chocolate is a memoir in essays beginning in the American Midwest and ending in north central Italy. In sharply rendered vignettes, Rick Bailey reflects on donuts and ducks, horses and car crashes, outhouses and EKGs. He travels all night from Michigan to New Jersey to attend the funeral of a college friend. In a trattoria in the hills above the Adriatic, he ruminates on the history and glories of beans, from Pythagoras to Thoreau, from the Saginaw valley to the Province of Urbino.

Bailey is a bumbling extra in a college production of *Richard III*. He is a college professor losing touch with a female student whose life is threatened by her husband. He is a father tasting samples of his daughter's wedding cake. He is a son witnessing his aging parents' decline. He is the husband of an Italian immigrant who takes him places he never imagined visiting, let alone making his own. At times humorous, at times bittersweet, Bailey's ultimate subject is growing and knowing, finding the surprise and the sublime in the ordinary detail of daily life.

RICK BAILEY is a professor emeritus of English at Henry Ford College in Michigan. He is the author or editor of several books on writing, including *The Creative Writer's Craft*.

University of Nebraska Press
Lincoln NE 68588-0630
nebraskapress.unl.edu

ISBN 978-1-4962-0119-5   US $19.95